THE TEN COUNT

HOWARD DARWIN'S REMARKABLE LIFE IN OTTAWA

JEFF DARWIN

Copyright © 2015 by Jeff Darwin

All rights reserved.

No part of this publication may be reproduced, distributed, or transmitted in any form or by any means, including photocopying, recording, or other electronic or mechanical methods, without the prior written permission of the publisher, except in the case of brief quotations embodied in critical reviews and certain other noncommercial uses permitted by copyright law.

Wholesale discounts for book orders are available through Ingram Distributors.

ISBN
978-1-987985-77-1 (softcover)
978-1-987985-75-7 (hardcover)
978-1-987985-76-4 (ebook)

Published in Canada.

First Edition

TABLE OF CONTENTS

I — THE TEN COUNT — *(Ottawa, 1937)* 1

II - BECOMING A NEWSBOY 7

III - THE WAR YEARS 19

IV - A NEW TEN COUNT 33

V - SOMEONE IN HIS CORNER 45

VI — PUTTING DOWN ROOTS 59

VII — PIPED TELEVISION 73

VIII — MAJOR JUNIOR 'A' HOCKEY 81

VIX — NO CONTEST: LOUIS VS. NELSON 97

X - CORNERMEN HAVE THEIR SAY 107

XI — THE OTTAWA LYNX 115

XII - RETIREMENT 127

XIII – STANDING EIGHTS 137

XIV - ONES THAT GOT AWAY 145

XV - THE NEWSBOY AND THE NEWSMEN 153

APPENDIX A – *Awards & Recognition* 165

APPENDIX B – *Photo Credits* 171

APPENDIX C – *People and Places* 173

ACKNOWLEDGEMENTS 185

"DARWIN, Howard (entrepreneur); b. 10 Sep 1931, Ottawa, Ont.; given name: Howard Joseph; m. Constance Goudie; c. Kim, Nancy, Jack, Jeff; ret'd. jeweler; 30-35 amateur bouts Beaver Boxing Club; switched to refereeing, promoting fights, managing fighters; promotions included wrestling, closed-circuit TV boxing matches; invested in Jr. A hockey with formation Ottawa 67's, part-owner; purchased London Gardens, London Jr. A hockey team; remained in hockey through '98; brought Triple A baseball Lynx to Ottawa '93; IL exec. of '95; sold Lynx '00; 1 Memorial Cup; 1 IL championship team; Ottawa ACT Earl Bullis Achievement award '98; ex-trustee Ottawa Sports Hall of Fame; mem. Ottawa Sports Hall of Fame; res. Ottawa, Ont."

FERGUSON, BOB: 'WHO'S WHO IN CANADIAN SPORT – 4th EDITION'; PG. 103

Howard Joseph Darwin was in reality born on September 10, *1930* (one year earlier than he often stated and was generally reported). He died on October 22, 2009 at 79 years of age, and this biography is dedicated to his memory.

The full-length version of Howard Darwin's amazing story, as told to his family and friends over the years, is lovingly detailed to the best of our abilities on the pages that follow. We hope that you will enjoy The Ten Count.

I – THE TEN COUNT
(OTTAWA, 1937)

The pickup basketball game was just underway at the old St. Patrick's Hall, and Howard Darwin was doing his best to keep up with a rag-tag bunch of older boys. Howard had pulled his long wool socks up over his trouser cuffs to free up his feet a little, but the worn leather hand-me-down shoes from 'goodness knows where', weren't helping matters. It was hardly basketball attire, but Howard was used to making due, being hungry, looking threadbare. Even as a six year-old, Howard used these feelings to more than hold his own with the larger, older kids - and even adults sometimes - he was growing up fast. He wanted to grow up fast. And Mayme, Howard's beloved mother, was usually finding a way to put things in perspective; to give her kids some hope; some sense of normal.

And it was hot - really hot on July 10, 1937 at the Ottawa Boys Club on Laurier Avenue. There was no way though that Howard was going to give in to his own sweat and the taller, faster boys just yet - because he was happy to be at the Boys Club - he felt safe and secure here. The Club had all kinds of organized activities and Howard loved them all, especially the boxing ring and donated gear. The youngest boys like Howard were not yet allowed to lace up the boxing gloves and settle the latest school yard spat with a few supervised rounds in the ring. Instead, the youngest kids would gather around the ring and cheer for their favourite, or just for the boy from their own street. And when there was a knock down or a slip, these pugilistic wannabes would shout The Ten Count together at the top of their lungs!

This was a rare summer Saturday where Howard had gotten away from the house early without his younger brother Rupert in tow. And now Miss Cameron was at the gym doors.

Howard knew that Miss Cameron was keeping an eye on him - and he didn't mind that at all. She was officially Fred McCann's secretary at the Ottawa Boys Club for these many 'boys at risk', but everyone knew that she meant so much more to all the underprivileged kids that found safe haven at 79 Laurier Avenue West. Howard understood that his family was poor - probably really poor - but he had no idea at that time that he was already one of 'Fred's boys'. Miss Cameron understood, and she recalled many years later that *"Howard was one of my favourites"*.[1]

Effie Cameron was only working at the Ottawa Boys Club that weekend because Fred McCann was already up at Mink Lake near Eganville, overseeing the installation of electricity to the sleeping cabins at his Camp Minwassin. Each summer Miss Cameron would herd very excited groups of 'Fred's Boys' over the Laurier Avenue bridge and up Nicholas Street, to Union Station to board a Canadian Pacific Railway train for their first train ride to their first summer camp experience at the Ottawa Boys Club's Camp Minwassin. Mink Lake had already become a pretty special place for thousands of the poorest kids in Ottawa since 1924.

Maybe THIS would be Howard's year for two-weeks at the Camp! He had been asking about it over and over, but all Miss Cameron had asked him so far was if he could swim yet? Of course he could! Howard's older brother Jack had taught him to swim LAST summer at Britannia Beach, and even brother Percy egged him into jumping into the Rideau Canal with him as a short cut home just two weeks ago. (picture I1, pg. 5) Howard made it all the way across from the end of Somerset Street to 'his' side of the canal without any help - although Percy had to hold both of their shirts and shoes up over his head!

Miss Cameron finally called Howard over, but she looked at him very differently today, and said to him: 'Go home right away Howard'.

Howard pulled his pant legs out of his socks and headed out the door and down the stairs into the sticky July afternoon at the foot of the Laurier Avenue Bridge. (picture I2, pg. 5) He scooted across Laurier and turned east up the bridge incline. At the crest of this southernmost crossing point for the canal and the railway tracks, Howard could see that he was now past the slow moving water below, and was starting over the first of the ten or so tracks and sidings that fanned out northward into the rail sheds just below Union Station. (picture I3, pg. 5) He recognized the Canadian National cars, the Canadian Pacific cars, and the distinctive cars of the New York Central Railroad – his father's line - his 'Old Man'. Howard couldn't remember if the Old Man was in town this weekend or still on the road. It didn't matter much, he was rarely home, and that was okay with Howard too.

Looking south from the bridge, Howard could just start to see the line of dilapidated row house tenements on Nicholas Street that marked 'his' neighbourhood – perhaps the toughest in Ottawa at the time. The paint had long since peeled or faded off the stretch of low rent clapboard dwellings, and this was his home. (picture I4, pg. 5) Skid Row. As he crossed over to the east side of the tracks – some said the 'wrong side' of the tracks in these dirty-thirties in Ottawa – he picked up the pace a little on the eastern down slope of the bridge. Howard knew that he had always had a lot of freedom to wander the streets of Ottawa - because he had older brothers who had even tougher friends and they always kept watch over the younger ones from Nicholas Street. Although the Ottawa Boys Club was a safe haven for all, it was still in Centretown, but now he was descending into his own neighbourhood. Howard's neighbourhood was not quite as nice as working class Sandy Hill or Eastview on his side of the tracks, but he knew it well and he knew every one of the older kids down here that he needed to know to avoid getting roughed up.

Howard hung a right onto Nicholas Street and started to jog south as he remembered Jack's bicycle was on the front step this morning. It was Saturday, Jack would be home today – no telegrams to deliver on Saturday! (picture I5, pg. 5) Maybe Jack would have the fare for them today for the streetcar, and Mayme could take them all to the western end of the line – to Britannia Beach! It was so much fun to get out of the city and it was really, really hot today. Howard was running home now.

Further down Nicholas Street something didn't look right. Howard could see now that their front door was open and there were adults coming and going from 291 Nicholas Street. He was running flat out and could already see his neighbour Mrs. Goulet coming out of the house and Mr. Foo and Mrs. Vieux heading in.

Howard ran past the neighbours, into the house and his brother Jack's arms. "Mayme is dead" Jack whispered. Howard Darwin was effectively on his own at age six, with the death of his mother Marie Albertine Darwin (nee Thivierge), that sweltering Saturday, July 10, 1937. (picture pg. 6)

Many years later Howard would explain to his wife Connie, how his recollections of the day his mother died formed his lifelong and unwavering aversion to cats. Howard told Connie that he could recall seeing his dead mother stretched out on a bed in full view of the kitchen where the adults where gathered quietly that fateful day, and seeing that there was a stray cat that had wandered in from the street lying across his Mayme's chest.

Mayme was waked the following day in Lowertown at the F. J. Hamon and Son Funeral Home at 136 Cobourg Street, and her funeral service was held at St. Joseph's Church in Sandy Hill early on Monday, July 12, 1937. Howard also recalled his family's annoyance from the day of his mother's funeral, when the Orangemen's Day Parade lingered on Laurier Avenue in front of their church – deliberately delaying the small funeral cortege from entering – at least until the bars opened for the Orangemen. Mayme was interred in the Darwin family plot at Ottawa's Notre Dame Cemetery in Eastview with only her father-in-law John Joseph Darwin (1856 – 1915), who had been laid to rest there many years earlier. She was just forty-seven years old, and her children believe she had died from untreated cervical cancer; simply because they were poor. Mayme left behind Howard's father Thomas Vincent Darwin ('Vince') aged 47, sister Josephine aged 19, brothers Jack 17, and Percy 12, and baby Rupert only 3 years old. Howard Darwin was just 6 years old when his beloved mother died.

(1) Winston, Iris: '200,000 Smiles' (75 Years at the Boys and Girls Club of Ottawa-Carleton), 1998 -pg. 35

THE TEN COUNT

Picture I6: "Mayme"; Marie Albertine Darwin (nee Thivierge) 1890-1937

II – BECOMING A NEWSBOY

With a heavy heart in September of 1937, Howard Darwin started his formal education in grade one at St. Joseph's Boys School. Howard missed his mother terribly, and was very fortunate to be taken in by his first teacher; Miss Burke. Miss Burke already knew of Howard's home situation and about his recent loss, and she stepped up and into his life when he needed it most. Howard felt that Miss Burke 'saved him' in grade one; she understood Howard and she understood his plight. It was Miss Burke who caught Howard Darwin's early attention and instilled and accelerated his natural curiosity for current affairs - while teaching him his trademark cursive writing style and penmanship - just as she would do for Rupert some three years later. Miss Burke had an enormous and early impact on Howard because she truly cared about him and would always check on him when he wasn't at school (often he was at home looking after Rupert), throughout his elementary school career at St. Joe's Boys School.

Miss Burke even took note when Howard didn't look well, and one time noticed that he had a swollen cheek. Once she had convinced him to let her look in his mouth, and confirmed that he was in a lot of pain (and had never been to a dentist), she scrounged around in her purse for a dollar, and generously sent Howard to her own dentist to have the infected tooth pulled. The alternative would have been finding a nickel to take the streetcar to the Civic Hospital in the west end to have the tooth pulled at the free clinic there.

On his seventh birthday on Friday, September 10, 1937, Howard was both surprised and delighted when both Miss Burke – whom he had known for less than two weeks - and his sister Josephine, remembered him with birthday cards. Howard decided then that he would get back on his feet again and beat The Ten Count this time.

By the time that Howard Darwin graduated from St. Joseph's in grade eight on June 15, 1945, Miss Burke had become the Principal of Centretown's only Catholic elementary boy's school. Not surprisingly, Howard Darwin never seemed to get in as much trouble in school as his equally guilty classmates. Howard could do no wrong in Principal Burke's eyes. From the time that Howard was able to afford it, until Miss Burke's passing many, many years later, Howard exchanged cards with her - and he always sent her a flower arrangement for Christmas.

St. Joe's was a brief daily reprieve for Howard Darwin from picking up or dropping off baby brother Rupert from one neighbour or another. With the weight of the world on their shoulders and 'Rupe' usually in tow, Howard or Percy would inevitably head over to the Ottawa Boys Club where Miss Cameron or Mr. McCann would help out with a few hours of activity for their baby brother. The Darwin brothers spent a lot of time at the Boys Club, and Howard remained grateful for that his entire life. (II1, pg. 16)

Following the death of their Mayme, the Darwin children understood that they had to fend for themselves, they had to grow up quickly, and they had to earn some money for food and clothing. Josephine (age 19) was already a live-in 'Mother's Helper' for the Cardell family at 13 Willow Street, Jack (age 17) was tending and training dogs for the RCMP, and Percy (age 12) got brother Jack's old job delivering telegraphs on his bicycle for the local Canadian Pacific Telegraph and Cable office. For his first enterprise, Howard Darwin (now seven-years-old) took to shining shoes on the sidewalks of Centretown for a nickel per pair. Rupert, only three, simply ran around after his older brothers.

The Old Man was home even less now. Without a word to any of his children, Vince Darwin would often pop an old toothbrush in his shirt pocket, hop a New York Central train as the Brakeman and disappear for weeks at a time. No clothes, no baggage, no worries. It was during these times from 1937 to 1939, that Howard Darwin later told his family with humiliation and some embarrassment, that he sometimes resorted to begging for food for Rupert and himself from his neighbours on Skid Row. These were the neighbours that the kids gossiped about; if you tended to swear, you were told that you "had a mouth like Mrs. Vieux!" and if your house was untidy you were "dirty like Mrs. Curry!", yet these same neighbours made sure that their own meager provisions were shared with the 'orphan' Darwin boys.

The poorest Ottawa families at the time seemed to Howard to be Irish – the "Micks" - like the Berrys, who lived nearby on King Edward Avenue. Jack Berry who was Percy's age, and Jimmy Berry who was Howard's age, tended to protect the Darwin boys in a very tough neighbourhood. Even the Goulet boys; Leo, Tony, Robert, Aime and Maurice – a full 'hockey line' living with their parents George and Anna Goulet at 271 Nicholas Street – knew enough not to mess with the Berry brothers (and the Darwin boys by extension). Anna and George Goulet were true 'silver cross' parents with all five of their courageous sons later serving overseas in World War II.

The impoverished neighbourhood family that Howard Darwin seemed to be most drawn to as a boy however, lived in a run-down unit in the lane behind the Darwins on Nicholas Street. The three Barre sisters comprised an extended French family who raised ducks and chickens for food on the patch of dirt in front of their house. Each Barre sister was raising her own children in that same little row-house alone, and there was not one father living there with them at the time. Some of Howard's closest childhood friends, like Carl "Bates" O'Leary, Eddie and Jack Lindsay, and Earl "Smokey" Davis were children of the Barre sisters living in the lane just behind them.

How tough was Nicholas Street? An Ottawa Sun new millennium poll of the 'toughest Ottawa street fighters of all time' ranked Jack Berry as the fifth toughest of them all; ranked right behind the infamous Gerry Barber (of the 'Chaud'), Frankie Cosenzo, Butch Lamoureux, and Paddy Post. [2] Howard Darwin always maintained that Jack Berry was the toughest of them all though, and further, that even Gerry Barber would have nothing to do with the Berrys in the 1940s. Nicholas Street was indeed a tough neighbourhood to grow up in. (II2, pg. 16)

Vince Darwin was a mean spirited alcoholic and the younger Darwin boys knew to stay away from him, particularly when he was drinking. They also knew that they needed to fend for themselves. On one occasion Percy reached for a broom to clobber a large rat in their kitchen, while the Old Man deftly grabbed the rat in his bare hands and broke its neck to show his frightened children how it should be done. Another morning in particular, when Jack and Percy were serving overseas, Howard woke his father to tell him that there was no food in the house and that Rupert was hungry. The Old Man got dressed and left the house angry. Vince returned home drunk that evening, and tossed a package of wieners at Howard and said: *"Here, go feed your lousy guts!"*

In 1942, Rupert broke his wrist 'hitching' behind an ice truck in the winter. Fearing a beating for Rupert, Howard tightly wrapped Rupert's wrist with a strip of leather to fashion a cast, and told his little brother to keep quiet about it. A few days later and now unable to tolerate the pain and swelling, Rupert reported the break to the Old Man and both boys got a beating for it.

The Old Man was also known to sell cheap sherry to other alcoholics on Sundays when liquor was not available anywhere in Ottawa (he was a Sunday bootlegger). Once when Vince was away for an extended period with the railway, Howard got an idea to make some food money. Howard and Rupert got up early on that Sunday morning and 'acquired' some ice to put the Old Man's sherry on. It didn't take too long before the Old Man's customers came around 'thirsty', and Howard & Rupert sold the chilled bottles for a nickel more that particular morning, over the protests of their father's regular customers! The boys replaced the sherry and pocketed a few extra coins – and got beaten when the Old Man came home and his customers told him what his youngest sons had done while he was away. (II3, pg. 16)

From a happier occasion around this time, Howard later recalled collecting bulrushes down near Dutchie's Hole in Sandy Hill. The boys would soak the bulrushes in kerosene 'acquired' from the rail yards below Nicholas Street, and use them as torches for their nighttime adventures. As each boy set about pulling and stacking their own bunch of bulrushes, Howard noticed a long snake slithering into his own pile which caused him to declare their work done for the day. Howard then graciously offered to carry a much larger pile of bulrushes for his friend, who would in turn carry Howard's very small bunch back to Nicholas Street – it was a great offer. Following closely behind his friend with the big snake inside the small bunch of bulrushes on his shoulder, Howard could barely contain his giggles as the snake slithered inside his friend's collar and down his shirt! That score was likely settled later in the boxing ring at the Ottawa Boys Club. (II4, pg. 16)

Howard Darwin's favourite back-alley and school yard pastimes included competitive marbles (or "alleys" as Howard called them), and craps. As a boy Howard was rarely without his growing bag of marbles or his lucky dice.

Another welcome distraction for young Howard and 'baby' Rupert during these very difficult years, was when their aunt Violet Connelly (sister of Mayme), or their older cousin Nola Connelly (daughter of Violet), would invite the boys to their hotel in Montreal: The Hotel Laurier at 1232 Dorchester Street near the bus station. Violet and Nola recognized the dire circumstances that the boys were in, and would often send them bus money to escape Nicholas Street for a few days to get their clothes mended and to get some proper food into them. Violet's husband William was recognized as the owner of this hotel in Montreal, but as Howard learned years later – but still failed to understand - the hotel was owned in reality by a local Jewish businessman and only managed by the Connellys who were living on site. This arrangement was more publicly acceptable in the anti-Semitic days of 1930s Montreal. It was here with his cousins that Howard first experienced the wonders of butter, fresh vegetables and even television.

As an adult, Howard Darwin was always fastidious about his clothes and his shoes – always the best that he could find or afford. All his life Howard could never pass by a fellow shoe-shine boy on the street wherever he was in the world, and when shoe-shine boys fell out of favour years later in Ottawa, he would routinely shine his own shoes at the kitchen table on Malone Crescent. Even at the age of seven, Howard understood the importance of good customer service and he was always thinking ahead about how he could make more money (and tips!). Howard would always ask his shoe shine customers how they made their own money, and ask for their advice on how he might do that too.

Around the same time Howard began helping out an older neighbourhood kid named Norman Traversy, who had a downtown corner for selling newspapers. (II5, pg. 16) With Traversy, Howard read (and sold) newspapers – cover to cover – everyday, and he continued to shine shoes too. He was now 'ink-stained'. This began Howard Darwin's lifelong love affair with current events and newspapers in general. At some points in his later life, Howard was reading up to six daily papers from around the world – he could (and did) talk to 'anyone' and 'everyone' about 'anything' - by the time he was seven years old. Other than a rare biography of someone he knew or had met, Howard Darwin was never known to read books his entire life. It was reading newspapers that first allowed a seven year old to escape Skid Row in his imagination, and follow his childhood idols around the world: band leader Louis Armstrong, and a humble giant of a prize fighter nicknamed 'The Brown Bomber'. Howard idolized The Brown Bomber, also known as Joe Louis, for his tenacity in beating his own formidable Ten Counts - again and again.

By the summer of 1938 tensions were running high in Europe following Germany's annexation of Austria five months earlier. German Chancellor Adolf Hitler was predicting that the June rematch of Max Schmeling and Joe Louis at Yankee Stadium for the world heavyweight boxing title would serve as further 'proof' to the world of the Nazi Party's (twisted) 'Arian Superiority' ideology (Louis had lost to Schmeling in their first fight in a 12th round knock-out in 1936). From his street corner at the intersection of Elgin and Lisgar, the young shoe shine boy kept his eyes on the rest of the world, and now he sensed an even better business opportunity. (II6, pg. 17) From the world news he was reading daily, and the increased military-issue footwear showing up on his shoe-shine box, Howard Darwin knew that it was only a matter of time before the headquarters building of the Royal Canadian

Navy on Elgin Street would be getting very busy. So the seven-year-old began pestering one of his regular shoe-shine customers, Percy Nelles, for an 'interview'. Finally - Mr. Nelles must have got tired of being asked - so he told young Howard to come and see him at his office the next day.

Interview preparations were intense that night. For this business proposition Howard had to look the part of the businessman that he was to become – but he had no suitable clothes. So, he borrowed a pair of Navy-issue woolen trousers, washed them carefully in the sink, rolled up the pant legs, and hung them as straight as possible behind the stove to dry (there was no iron on Nicholas Street of course). Next was a jacket – no luck there – so he also washed his best looking top; a Toronto Maple Leafs hockey sweater. (II7, pg. 17) The last item was shoes, however the best looking ones in the house would be on the feet of his older brothers the next day, so Howard made do with slip-on winter 'toe-rubbers', held onto his socking feet with some 'new' elastic bands he had been saving.

The next day Howard Darwin, aged seven and now properly attired, marched smartly into Naval Defense Headquarters (wearing toe rubbers over his socks), for his meeting with Vice Admiral Percy W. Nelles, Commander of the Royal Canadian Navy and Chief of the Naval Staff. His proposition? To set up a news stand *inside* the lobby of the building to sell the evening Ottawa Journal and the Ottawa Citizen newspapers after school, at three-cents apiece – and he wanted *exclusivity*. And it worked – he was soon building exclusive before he started grade two!

May of 1939 brought very exciting news to eight-year-old Howard Darwin: King George VI and Queen Elizabeth I (by then the Queen Mother), were coming to Ottawa, and their Royal Train would be pulling into town right through Howard's neighbourhood! It was the first time that a reigning monarch had visited Canada and it was a huge event for a city and country still in the throes of economic depression. The King would dedicate the new National War Memorial that all the neighbourhood kids had watched being constructed for months now at the Connaught Place square (nicknamed Confusion Square at the time; picture II10, pg. 17), and the Cameron Highlanders of Ottawa would receive the King's and Regimental Colours from their own Regimental Colonel-In-Chief, King George VI himself, on Parliament Hill. King George and Queen Elizabeth would meet in Canada for pre-war alliance talks with Prime Minister Mackenzie King - and later in their tour - with President F. D. Roosevelt in the United States.

While the rest of Howard's grade three classmates made signs and 'Long Live the King' banners to greet the historic Royal Tour of North America, Howard schemed about how he was going to get from his front door, across the street, down the embankment and onto the King's train to meet The Man himself, before the big mucky-mucks met his train at Union Station. And it all worked out - except for his timing.

On the much anticipated Ottawa arrival day of the Royal Train, Howard and another boy easily worked their way down into the familiar rail yards between Nicholas Street and the Rideau Canal, and there they were! The most majestic parlor cars they had ever seen behind an oversized engine emblazoned with 'Canada' on each side. But there wasn't a soul around; no Kings, no Queens, no Attendants in Waiting, no staff, no guards, no soldiers – no one. Unfortunately for these boys, the Royals had switched out of the train at a specially erected station at Island Park Drive, and continued their procession to Rideau Hall in an open, horse drawn carriage! So, the boys did what boys do when they're alone in places they shouldn't be – they clamored up, into and all through the open Royal Parlour cars – and 'acquired' a box of the King's cornflakes as their trophy! When Howard caught up with his classmates and 100,000 other Canadians later that week for the opening of the National War Memorial, he bragged mightily about what he had already seen of the Royal Tour!

With the outbreak of the war in September 1939, the traffic through the Naval Defense Headquarters building was huge and the appetite for news from Europe was insatiable. Howard was by then making a small fortune selling over one thousand newspapers a day at three cents apiece - sometimes netting $10 on a good day, (Howard's gross profit per paper sold was nine tenths of a cent). That's about $170 in today's dollars 'tax free' – not bad for three hours work from a nine year old after school! Adult unemployment in Ottawa was over 20% and the average adult wage was between 60 and 90 cents per hour in 1939. Howard's biggest expense was buying the ten wagons each year that he used to haul his newspapers to his stand every afternoon – they wore out quickly. During World War II, Howard was making more from his newsstand than his father was making, *when* the Old Man was working, and even more than the men serving overseas. In an October 6, 1943 letter home to his father from the front, older brother Jack Darwin even weighed in by asking: *"Has Howard still got his paper round. He certainly would be foolish to sell it for fifty bucks when he is making 15 to 20 dollars a week. It is certainly nice money. It is not easy to pick up that much money even during peace time."*

Howard told the story of his patron, Commander Nelles, stopping to buy his regular paper one afternoon and having only a nickel with him. Always the entrepreneur, Howard feigned that he had no pennies left himself for change that afternoon and the Commander said *"That's okay Howard. See you tomorrow"*. Howard bragged heartily to his brothers that night about copping such a huge tip on a single newspaper! The next afternoon however, Commander Nelles stopped by for his regular three-cent newspaper, and handed Howard only a single penny in full payment – lesson learned.

And what does a nine-year-old in Ottawa do with a small fortune from his cash business during the war years? Well, he bought food and clothing for Rupert, cigarettes for his brothers overseas, and then lots of new dress shoes and suits of course! For the rest of his life, Howard Darwin maintained that selling newspapers was the best job that he ever had. (II8 & II9, pg. 17)

(2) McRae, Earl: The Ottawa Sun; pg. 7, Dec 19, 1999

JEFF DARWIN

THE TEN COUNT

III - THE WAR YEARS

By the summer of 1939 the Ottawa Boys Club had brought out a club mascot (what we would today call a 'therapy dog'), in the form of Fred McCann's little Scottish Terrier named "Tammy" - plus a new Facilities Manager named Harry Johnson. Mr. Johnson's crippled leg would keep him out of World War II, and he became a father figure to many boys whose own fathers went into the service of their country between 1939 and 1945. Harry Johnson literally opened doors for Howard, usually to the gym or to the billiards room upstairs after hours. Johnson could size up the bored boys who had dropped in at 79 Laurier Avenue West and put together a pick-up game of just about anything to keep them occupied and off the streets. For Howard Darwin, and later younger brother Rupert, Mr. Johnson was both understanding and stern when necessary, and he became a father figure when they needed it most throughout the war years in Ottawa. (III1, pg. 30)

When Howard and Rupert made it to Camp Minwassin in the summer of one of the war years, there was a teenaged Boys Club camp counsellor named Dougie Thompson working at the camp who made a favourable impression on them both. "Officer Doug Thompson" of the Ottawa Police would later kept a sympathetic eye on the Darwin boys throughout their troubled teenaged and young adult lives, and finally a retired "Pops" Thompson shared the bar-rail on occasion with Howard Darwin at the Ottawa Nepean Canadians Sports Club. Ottawa seemed smaller then. The Ottawa Nepean Canadians Sports Club was another place where all were welcome and where many, like Howard, felt that they belonged in their later years.

Tensions continued to build through the summer of 1939 in Ottawa, and war in Europe seemed inevitable to Howard. On July 23, 1939 Mahatma Gandhi, the spiritual leader of India, wrote a personal letter to Adolf Hitler imploring Hitler to cease his territorial aggression and avoid another world war. Gandhi's letter and the diplomatic efforts of other world leaders such as Mackenzie King that summer proved futile. Being a real newshound, nine-year-old Howard Darwin was already following these developments closely in the newspapers and on the radio at his every opportunity. During the war years in Ottawa, it was not unusual to encounter Prime Minister Mackenzie King out walking his dog unaccompanied along Laurier or King Edward Avenue, and Howard knew that he was somehow witnessing history - and he would need to remember it all.

World War II broke out in earnest with Germany's invasion of Poland on September 1, 1939. Howard's nineteen-year-old brother Jack went immediately to the Landsdowne Park Army Induction Centre to volunteer with the Cameron Highlanders of Ottawa. On September 11, 1939, Jack began his basic Army training at the Beaver Barracks in Ottawa, and later that winter, in Borden, Ontario. (III2, pg. 31) Brother Percy was fourteen now and vowing to follow brother Jack into the Service. Nine-year-old Howard, now in grade three, was unusually engaged in news and world affairs for a boy his age. Howard Darwin had grown up fast.

In July of 1940, the men of the First Battalion of the Cameron Highlanders quietly reassembled at the Beaver Barracks at Landsdowne Park in Ottawa, and Howard was one of the first to learn 'from the street' that his brother Jack was back in town. The soldiers were sequestered in their barracks as preparations were made for their Passing Out Parade where some 800 young Ottawa natives would be shipped initially to Iceland, and then directly into harm's way in Europe. The evening before the parade, a stove pipe fire started in a neighbouring row house which quickly spread to the top floor of the Darwin's home. Fire crews from the King Edward and Laurier Avenue station extinguished the blaze, but not before the roof was completely burnt off of 291 Nicholas Street on Skid Row.

On Passing Out Day, Howard took up position just below the new National War Memorial in sight of the parade route down from Parliament Hill. Howard was determined (for some forgotten reason) to inform his older brother Jack about the fire at their home before he shipped out. When Jack Darwin marched into view, Howard sprinted into the street and jogged beside his older brother who was marching in formation with his unit: *"Jack! Jack! The house burnt down last night!"* Howard blurted out. Brother Jack was barely able to acknowledge his little brother that day, and nine-year-old Howard carried the guilt of his last spoken words and the last sight of his older brother in July 1940.

Jack Darwin wrote home often, and he maintained a keen interest in the fate of his younger brothers Percy, Howard and Rupert (Josephine was already on her own), throughout World War II. Jack was sending most of his Army pay home during the war to their father Vincent for the support of the boys - although it was obvious from the frustration expressed in some of his letters that the funds rarely made it past the Old Man to the care of his younger brothers on Nicholas Street. In a letter to the Old Man written by Jack from Iceland on August 28, 1940, Jack wrote: *"So Mable moved out to (sic) bad. I sort of expected that she would. Although I had no love for her."* Jack's letter was in reference to one of his father's girlfriends and drinking partners who had moved into 291 Nicholas Street shortly after the boys' mother died.

As the war dragged on into the summer of 1941, the number of healthy Canadian males eighteen years or older who were eligible and willing to volunteer for World War II service had declined significantly. Enlistment standards were falling at the induction centres and the Navy was now openly accepting seventeen-year-olds. Armed with this knowledge, Percy Darwin joined the Royal Canadian Navy using a letter signed by 'Vincent Darwin' agreeing to allow his 'sixteen-year-old son' to volunteer at the earliest, exceptional age then allowed with parental permission. Percy was only fifteen-years-old. The Old Man was out of town; the letter was forged. Older brother Percy had now made it off of Skid Row too - leaving just Howard (not yet eleven years old) and Rupert (age six) to truly fend for themselves. (III3, pg. 31)

Although he had escaped Nicholas Street himself, Percy also kept in touch with Howard and Rupert during the war. In an early, unsettling letter written home directly to Howard from the dockyards in Halifax, Percy wrote: *"I hear your (sic) saving millions, it's (sic) just as well because it will come in handy sometime, or should I say all the time. Is Rupe still helping you with the papers?...The fellow that sleeps in the next bed to me shot himself the other morning, you might of read something about it in the Ottawa papers...hope to hear from you soon, till then take care of yourself and Rupe. Your Kid Brother (sic) Percy."*

By the fall of 1941 it was apparent that eleven-year-old Howard Darwin might be on the path to 'juvenile delinquency' as it was then known. In a stern letter home on October 26, 1941 from his eldest brother Jack with the 'Canadian Army Overseas', Jack wrote:

"Dear Howard & Rupert. Received your most welcome letter dated Sept 21. I was sure glad to hear from you. I thought that you forgot about me altogether. I am glad to hear that both of you are well. As for myself I am feeling swell. Well Howard I am sorry to hear about Rupert hurting himself. I am glad he is alright now. You should keep a better eye on him. After all your (sic) the boss at home now. What's this I heard about you not passing your exams last June? I was certainly surprised to hear that. You can't be studying very hard. What about promising me that you will try to study a lot this year and then you won't have to stay two years in the same class. You really can be smart if you want to. I know that you always had a good report card when I was home with you. What's the trouble anyways. Are you missing school to (sic) much. So you are a working man now eh! Nice going you will be able to keep yourself in small change now and get what you want. I know where the Aylmer Apts are. I used to deliver telegrams there often. How is everything going at home Howard. How do you and Rupert get along. Are you by yourself most of the time. I heard that Rupert and you had a swell time when you were in camp last summer. Have you still got my tent. I hope so. If you have you and Rupert can keep it for yourself. Well how is the rugby games coming along. I guess the season is well under way by now. Have you seen any games. Is Arnie Charbonneau playing this year. Percy must be getting along alright in the navy. Where is he now in Montreal yet or in

Halifax. I haven't heard from him yet. When you get the time Howard drop me a line whenever you can. I get more news from you & Rupert than I do from anybody else. I sure like getting letters from you. So don't forget eh. Well Howard I think I will close for tonight. Hoping to hear from you shortly. Give my love to Rupert and give him a big kiss for me and don't forget to look after him. Remaining as ever your loving brother, Jack XXX."

The war years in Ottawa were led municipally by the simple, steady hand of Ottawa's longest serving mayor, Stanley Lewis. Lewis was - like Howard - Ottawa-born and bred, and was a genial, self-made businessman and sports enthusiast who led his city as mayor from 1936 to 1948.

On December 4, 1941, Jack Darwin wrote to Howard and Rupert asking for a personal favour: *"Howard do you and Rupert want to go and see my girlfriend for me. She told me in her last letter that she thought that she met a boy who looks a lot like me. Maybe it is you. She lives at 577 Somerset St. W. Ottawa. Her name is Eileen Coghlan. If you go and see her be sure and look nice. Don't forget to let me know if you do go."* (III4, pg. 31)

The 1940 fire damage to the Darwin's low rent row house was not repaired by their landlord until the spring of 1942. This was because these derelict properties were already owned by the University of Ottawa and were slated for demolition for an expansion of Ottawa U to accommodate the anticipated influx of veterans as students after the war. A house without a roof on its top floor did prove amusing however for one of its poor tenants; ten-year-old Howard Darwin. The Darwins moved their few belongings not ruined by the smoke or water in the upstairs bedrooms, down to their ground floor. The upstairs - now 'outdoor' - toilet remained functional, albeit open to the elements, so they continued to do their business under a wide open sky. Howard recalled their open air toilet being quite peaceful, except when it snowed, and he and Rupert would need to carry up some newspaper to read and then to wipe themselves afterwards! A new form of entertainment even grew out of their upstairs predicament. While sitting on the toilet, the boys discovered that they could drop a baited hook on a long string down the abandoned stove pipe and 'fish' for the rats downstairs!

Percy Darwin's naval career was relatively short and heroic. Shortly after enlisting underage to escape Nicholas Street, Percy was deployed to the HMC Dockyard and HMCS Stadacona in Halifax for his training in 1941 until he got his permanent deployment to the newly commissioned HMCS Weyburn (K173), a corvette class convoy escort ship for the Atlantic supply routes in 1942. In one of Percy's many letters home to Howard, Percy wrote in June of 1942: *"I hope you and Rupe pass this year. If you don't you can expect a blast from me boy."* In another letter directly to Howard and Rupert the next year, Percy described eight *"swell"* days of leave, that brother Percy (Navy) and brother Jack (Army), somehow managed to spend together in London, England in December 1942. It was the last time the two eldest Darwin boys would ever see each other.

In January 1943, the Weyburn moved to the Mediterranean off of North Africa where it was famously sunk by the Germans on February 22, 1943, killing twelve. *"Through seven trips from The Rock (of Gibraltar) to ports in Algiers and Tunisia, they had escorted convoys during the North African campaign. They'd survived hailstorms of fire from Axis dive-bombers, E-boats and submarines. They'd done it without casualty. Then, their work in the Mediterranean completed, they were heading for home on a bright, sunny, calm day when two U-boat torpedoes ripped them in the space of half an hour."* [3]

News from the war was usually delayed and heavily censored to avoid aiding the enemy. The first indication that something had happened to Percy and the Weyburn came on the afternoon of March 5, 1943, when a cryptic telegram was delivered to 291 Nicholas Street that simply said: "ALL WELL AND SAFE PLEASE DONT WORRY HOPE TO SEE YOU SOON PERCY DARWIN". The telegram was datelined Gibraltar 1, and by March 9th, more details of the Weyburn sinking were being published in the Ottawa newspapers. There were 71 survivors from the Weyburn, including a twice-torpedoed, seasoned naval veteran: eighteen-year-old Percy Darwin of 291 Nicholas Street, and fellow Ottawa boys: Cliff Potter (80 Arlington Ave), Roger Haspeck (136 Queen St), John Tasse (373 Lyon St), Lorenzo Charbonneau (49 ½ Friel St), Leo Rainville (234 Water St) and Reg Boucher (295 St. Patrick St). [4] The survivors of the Weyburn were back in Halifax in early April 1943, and Percy was taken directly to Rockhead Hospital in Halifax where his injuries were treated for over three months until he was medically discharged and back in Ottawa by late summer of 1943. (III5, pg. 31)

Because of the regular censorship of their letters, the older Darwin brothers overseas became adept at being quite unspecific about where they were and what military actions they had participated in. Also, when letters or packages failed to reach the front it was commonly assumed that they 'went down' during the crossing. On August 22, 1942 however, Jack Darwin wrote the following to the Old Man: *"What do you think about that raid on France the other day. I know quite a few chaps that went over but didn't come back. It's to (sic) bad our outfit didn't get a crack at it also. Maybe our turn is next though, who knows at least we are hoping to be in the next one."* Jack was speaking of course about the infamous Dieppe Raid, and the Camerons did of course get their own 'crack' at a big French raid in the summer of 1944 - by fighting their way ashore at Juno beach on D-Day.

The war years in Ottawa left many kids itching to join the fight taken up by their older brothers in Europe, and the boxing ring at the Ottawa Boys Club was very busy. One of those local older brothers was Harvey Lacelle who in 1940 defeated an up and coming American fighter by the name of Walker Smith, in Smith's last amateur bout in nearby Utica, N.Y.. Walker Smith then changed his name and turned pro. In 1942 twenty-three-year-old Pilot Officer Air Gunner Harvey Lacelle was killed when his Halifax bomber was shot down over Bremen, Germany. Walker Smith went on to earn an illustrious professional boxing career. The professional ring name that Smith chose after his last amateur defeat to Ottawa's own Harvey Lacelle was "Sugar Ray" Robinson!

By 1942 Howard Darwin had finally made it to the Ottawa Boys Club's Camp Minwassin on Mink Lake, and he had already fought in a couple of inter-club amateur boxing cards in Ottawa and Montreal. In Ottawa, boxing lessons and matches were being supervised at the Boys Club by (ex-army) Mel Swartman, but for the older, more serious boys like Howard and the younger Lacelle brothers Ronnie and Arnie, it didn't seem to be enough to keep them off the streets and out of trouble. The Gillette Razor Company had begun sponsoring live boxing on the radio, and many young boys just wanted to fight.

So in 1943 Joey Sandulo started the Beaver Boxing Club to help the more serious practitioners of the Sweet Science burn off their energy against teens from neighbouring towns and cities. The Beaver Boxing Club's record for keeping Ottawa's poor and tough kids out of trouble during the war years was remarkable. Joey Sandulo and Beaver Boxing produced Canadian Olympians Joey Sandulo himself (London 1948), and Clayton Kenny (Helsinki 1952), plus a number of successful, local professional boxers including Gale "Flash" Kerwin. Membership at the Beaver Boxing Club was open to boys aged twelve and up, and Howard, now aged twelve and in grade six, was one of the first kids through the door and into the ring in 1943.

While Howard Darwin's snooker and craps games seemed to be improving due to the Ottawa Boys Club, his personal ring record peaked during the war years, fighting an estimated twenty-five amateur fights between 1943 and 1945. Howard trained as a Featherweight, mostly under the tutelage of a very good local boxer (and later boxing referee) named Gordie Montagano. Also hanging around the Beaver Boxing Club at that time was Gordie's little brother Earl Montagano, who would later become Howard's longtime business partner. In a newspaper column in 1991, Howard reflected that: *"One thing you learn (in the ring) fast is that you're either good or no good, and I was no good...I guess I won a few, but I also got my beak broken three times. Once in Cornwall from this guy in the Merchant Navy. I was 13, he was 18. He stopped me. If I had a nickname, it was Canvas Back."* [5]

Howard Darwin's young life was already a series of knock-downs and hard lessons. His mother Mayme had been there to help him understand the death of his baby sister Johanna, who died just six weeks after coming into their lives when Howard was not quite three. Mary Johanna Darwin was born on June 10, 1932 and died on July 27, 1932 of meningitis. Miss Burke was there to help him beat The Ten Count at six-years-old, and the Ottawa Boys Club helped Howard beat the count until he was twelve, and then the Beaver Boxing Club surely saved him during the war years. There was always boxing, and Howard Darwin simply loved the fight game and its good people. Good people like Joe Louis: grandson of a slave and son of an Alabama sharecropper, who had scored a first round knock-out over Germany's

Max Schmeling for the World Heavyweight Championship at Yankee Stadium on June 22, 1938. With Louis's KO, democracy had won out over fascism; the Brown Bomber had defeated the Black Uhlan of the Rhine, and now boxing – just like Howard Darwin's view of the world – was perfectly colour-blind. Now Joe Louis – just like Howard's brother Jack – was serving his country in the Army too. Howard always looked up to his older brother Jack of course, but he was also trying to model his own adolescence after another personal hero in the character of the humble Brown Bomber. (III6, pg. 32)

Howard Darwin's St. Joseph's Boys School monthly report from Grade Seven in 1942 – 1943, paints an interesting picture of the twelve year old's scholastic focus at the time. The monthly teacher's comments were these: *"September: 'Not enough application'; October: '14th in the class out of 34'; November: 'Rank 17'; December: 'Can do better'; January: 'Improving'; February: 'Howard is doing much better'; March: 'Is there any reason why Howard should drop so far behind last month?'"* [6] The Grade Seven teacher's recorded comments on this report card stopped in March, which coincided with the parent's required monthly signatures on the back as well, although the 'Thos V Darwin' signature for March was clearly forged! Howard Darwin was nonetheless promoted to Grade Eight on June 22, 1943, with mostly 'Fair' and 'Unsatisfactory' ratings in the monthly General Progress section. (III7, pg. 32)

Early in 1943, Jack Darwin couldn't mask his pride for his twelve year old brother Howard back in Ottawa. In a letter home to his father, Jack wrote: *"By golly Howard must be quite a boy eh! I got a letter from him which was really good. A real business man if there ever was one. He was telling me about Rupe giving him a hand with the papers and helping to spend his 'dough'. I sure would like to see them."*

Despite having been continuously deployed for almost five years, Jack Darwin managed to keep an eye on his sister, and all three of his younger brothers back in Ottawa through letters. In May of 1944 Jack wrote to Howard: *"How is everything going with your papers. I suppose you are still making a few bucks a night out of it. Is Rupe still working for you. You must be growing like a bad weed. Do you still wear a hat. I don't suppose you bother about the girls eh! I heard a few rumours that you do but I don't believe it. You must be too busy working to do anything else."* To his father that same month Jack wrote: *"Rupe is sure the boy to save money, I didn't think he could do it. Howard is just the other way round, he can spend it as fast as myself. He's a real business man though."*

In a September 1944 letter to Percy, who was discharged from the Navy and was back on Nicholas Street by the fall of 1943 and looking for work, Jack expressed continued concern from the front about the younger boys. Jack wrote: *"I am certainly glad you are home to keep an eye on them. I have been wondering where Howard is going to go to school. Percy make sure he doesn't get any crazy ideas like you and I had of quitting school. After all it must be a lot harder on them growing up the better part of their life without a mother. They will have a inclination to do a lot on their own."* (III8, pg. 32)

In the fall of 1944, fourteen-year-old Howard Darwin started grade eight, and he simply couldn't stand it any longer – he had to get off Skid Row somehow. Howard studied every newspaper account and listened to every radio dispatch from France regarding the brave Canadians – including his brother Jack with the Cameron Highlanders of Ottawa - who had stormed the beaches of Normandy on the June 6, 1944 D-Day Invasion. Over 1,000 Canadians were killed on the D-Day offensive and nearly 2,000 other Canadians were injured - but not brother Jack so far.

Howard planned his own escape (after all, it had worked for Percy). With a forged 'father's permission letter' of his own for an 'underage enlistment', Howard briefly quit school and joined the Navy. A couple of weeks later, a uniformed, fourteen-year-old Howard Darwin met up with other new naval recruits at the Navy Induction Centre to get on a bus to the seven seas (via basic naval training in Kingston, Ontario), for the Allies final advance against Germany in Europe. Predictably, he was found out and was turned back before boarding the bus! Although Howard failed to make an underage escape from Skid Row like his brother Percy had, he did make the walk back to 291 Nicholas Street with his head held high and full of further schemes to get up and beat The Ten Count one more time. (III9, pg. 32)

On October 7, 1944, Jack Darwin sounded frustrated in a letter from the Front to his father saying: *"I am well over five years in the Army now. Here's hoping it won't last another five."* But to his brother Percy on

November 19, 1944, Jack wrote optimistically (from Holland) that: *"It should be over soon the way we are going now. I have been on German soil quite a few times and I wouldn't trade any of it for a little bit of Canada."* In response to a letter received from his fourteen-year-old, Navy volunteer reject and 'newshound' brother Howard Darwin, Jack wrote on November 25, 1944 that: *"I do hope that you look after him (Rupert). Yes you are right we are where you think we are (Holland). It's* (sic) *not a bad country but it still isn't as good as Canada. How would you and Rupe like to call around and see my girlfriend (Eileen Coghlan) and if possible take her to the show for me and I'll pay you back someday."*

The gloom in Jack's letters returned however with one to the Old Man on November 29, 1944 saying: *"There is some going home alright Dad but I am afraid it will be a long time before I'll make it. Here's hoping that the war doesn't last that long."*

In the final letter that fourteen-year-old Howard Darwin received from his eldest brother overseas dated December 12, 1944, Jack thanked Howard for the Christmas parcel and he asked if Howard thought that the Christmas tips from the newspapers would be 'any good this year'. Jack continued: *"It certainly will be a little different Xmas over here this year. When we were in England we could go around and see people whom we knew but here who wants to go across the line and wish the Germans a Merry Xmas. How is Rupe getting along. I understand he is running one of your paper stands for you. By golly! You must be rolling in the 'dough' now days."*

(3) Frayne, Trent: 'Returned Weyburn Men Describe Vessel's Loss' (The Globe and Mail – April 10, 1943)
(4) 'Canadian Corvette Weyburn Torpedoed Off North Africa' (The Ottawa Journal – March 9, 1943)
(5) McRae, Earl: 'A Passion for the Punchers' (The Ottawa Sun; pg. 39, February 17, 1991)
(6) Ingoldsby, A.: Grade 7 Teacher: St. Joseph's Boys School 'Ottawa Separate Schools Monthly Report'; Howard Darwin 1942 - 1943

*Picture III1: Ottawa Boys Club, 79
Laurier Ave. West in 1942 (left to right):
Henry Shorey, Earl Davis, Rupert Darwin, Howard Darwin
("Tammy" sitting on Howard's lap), Carl Barry and Gilbert Barlow.*

Jack Darwin, Percy Darwin, Howard and Rupert, Percy makes it back

JEFF DARWIN

IV – A NEW TEN COUNT

Following his failed underage enlistment bid the previous fall, January 1945 opened for Howard Darwin with more hopeful news from the Western Front reaching his newsstand each day - and his thoughts turned to the safe return of his older brother Jack. Howard had learned that his eldest brother had indeed survived coming ashore with the Cameron's at Juno Beach on D-Day the previous June - when Jack's outfit finally got their own 'crack at it' - and the Allies were now pressing inland quickly. The tide of the war in Europe was finally turning.

On a mild Tuesday afternoon, January 23, 1945, Howard answered a knock on the door of 291 Nicholas Street from a lone Canadian National Telegraph delivery boy, and signed for the dreaded telegram addressed to his father Thomas ('Vince') Darwin, informing the Old Man that his son, Company Sergeant-Major John (Jack) Joseph Darwin - Howard's eldest brother and personal hero - was killed in action on January 16, 1945 near Groesbeek, Holland. (pg. 40) The romanticized, Hollywood version of World War II notification of next of kin - is just that. There were no soldiers in uniform, no Army Chaplin and worst of all, no support of any kind for fourteen-year-old, devastated, Howard Darwin.

The sympathy letter that arrived at Nicholas Street a few days later from R. C. Army Chaplain, Donald A. Kerr, said that Kerr had last seen Jack Darwin on New Year's Day 1945, when Jack helped him to serve Mass in '...*the beautiful little Dutch Church...almost directly opposite his Coy HQ...*' and that another Canadian priest, Fr. Hickey, M.C. had taken Jack's body '...*back of the lines for burial in the temporary Cdn. Military Cemetery here, somewhere here in Holland.*' As was customary during the war, soldiers were buried quickly with their countrymen and as close as possible to where they fell. There was no Dutch funeral or Canadian service for Jack Darwin, however his memory and his remains continue to be gratefully watched over by the Dutch families that he helped to liberate near Groesbeek, Holland. (pg. 41)

Although World War II effectively ended for Howard when he signed for his brother Jack's death notice telegram in January, the beginning of the end for the rest of the world began with the surrender of Germany's troops in Holland (where Jack had fallen), on May 5, 1945. Germany's unconditional and overall surrender came early on May 7th, and when the news of Germany's defeat reached Ottawa that Monday morning pandemonium erupted on streets around the world, including the spontaneous celebrations in Ottawa's Uppertown. Howard ran into the streets around the war memorial and met up with his friends who had also skipped school on the news, whereupon he wisely recruited a few of them to pull countless wagon loads of newspapers for himself and Rupert for a record afternoon and evening of selling The Ottawa Citizen ("IT'S ALL OVER IN EUROPE! NAZI SURRENDER COMPLETE"), and The Ottawa Journal ("SURRENDER COMPLETE!") newspapers. (pg. 41)

The following day; Tuesday, May 8, 1945 was declared 'VE Day' by the King of the British Commonwealth, so Howard and Rupert dressed up with the masses to celebrate on an official 'no school' day - but missed Prime Minister Churchill's live radio address broadcast on CBO and CKCO in Ottawa while they sold thousands of newspapers as souvenirs that afternoon. They were both home and exhausted however in time to hear Prime Minister King's live radio address to the nation later that night. The celebrations in Ottawa were particularly bitter-sweet for Howard knowing that his brother Jack had been killed in action just 112 days before. (pg. 41)

After the war, Howard Darwin maintained his preoccupation with sports, world news and local current affairs. Howard was fascinated by the 'Gouzenko Affair' when Igor Gouzenko defected from the Soviet Union on September 5, 1945 in Ottawa with a briefcase full of documents on Russian spying activities around the world. Howard would later try to convince his neighbourhood friends to accompany him up Somerset Street to Dundonald Park, to sit on the *"very same park bench"* that the undercover RCMP officers had sat on in September, to watch as the KGB ransacked Gouzenko's apartment across the street at number 511 Somerset. Little did fifteen-year-old Howard know, that he was now also witness to the start of the Cold War.

As post war life in Ottawa slowly returned to normal, a major crime rocked Ottawa and mesmerized a teenaged Howard Darwin. In the early morning of October 24, 1945, Detective Thomas Stoneman of the Ottawa Police jumped out of his patrol car at Slater and O'Connor Streets to arrest three men who were breaking into cars near the Bytown Inn. A gun battle ensued, and Detective Stoneman became the first Ottawa policeman to be killed in the line of duty. For fifteen-year-old Howard Darwin this was huge local news that he simply could not resist witnessing firsthand. Along with a few of his classmates, Howard later skipped school to watch the final day of the murder trial of Eugene Larment of 350 Wellington Street from the public gallery, but was called down to the Principal's office at St. Pat's High School the next day to explain his absence. Howard's *"I had a cold"* excuse was quickly exposed as a lie when the Principal presented Howard with a picture of himself in the morning's newspaper from the court house doorway the previous day. (pg. 42) Howard was suspended from school once again - which simply gave him more time to hang out at the courthouse that winter!

Fittingly, Howard skipped school again on March 3, 1946. He climbed onto the porch roof of a friend's house across the street from the Carleton County Jail and peered over its stone walls into the courtyard to watch the hanging of Eugene Larment for the murder of Detective Thomas Stoneman. It was the last hanging in Ottawa's history, and fifteen-year-old Howard Darwin was there to see it firsthand.

Six days into Howard's second year of high school (grade ten) was Tuesday, September 10, 1946, and it was also Howard's sixteenth birthday. Age sixteen was the earliest any student could 'legally' sign themselves out of classes at St. Patrick's High School and Howard celebrated his special day by reporting to the Principal's Office to sign himself out of class – forever. With a grade nine education and loads of confidence and street smarts, Howard Darwin set out to beat the next Ten Count, and become a success - anywhere other than on Nicholas Street.

It wasn't long before Howard's job search brought him to a familiar stretch of Rideau Street, and Tim Burke Jewellers as a Watchmaker's Apprentice. Here Howard learned the jeweller's trade from end to end, gravitating towards the larger time pieces like carriage, mantel and grandfather clocks. Over the course of 1946 and 1947, Howard Darwin earned his Certified Watchmaker's papers, while scheming of ways to become his own boss – and make millions – someday.

The local watering hole favoured by working class men and young adults like Howard in those days was the Albion Hotel at 1 Daly Avenue beside the Courthouse and the Carleton County Jail. (pg. 43) The Albion was a lively place in the late 40s where lawyers, policemen and judges often mixed with those on trial next door, and even with the jurors who were sometimes sequestered overnight in the rooms upstairs. Originally built in 1844, the Albion Hotel was purchased by former NHL star Bill Touhey in August of 1946 for around $100,000. In 1946, the Albion was already Ottawa's oldest and most renowned hotel, holding down the fourth corner across from the police station, the courthouse, and the jail. (Touhey sold the hotel to Stanley Ages in 1971 for $900,000, and it was torn down in the mid-eighties.)

The Albion Hotel's 'Main' and 'Ladies' entrance was on Daly Avenue, and its 'Men Only' entrance for the busy lounge area was on Nicholas Street across from Charles Ogilvie's department store. The Nicholas Street entrance was naturally the most convenient for Howard and his older brother Percy and their neighbourhood friends, where they became well known to the Albion Hotel's owner, Bill Touhey.

It was at the Albion that Howard once watched a teary-eyed Jack Berry settle into his chair to enjoy his nickel dropped in the juke-box for the song "Danny-Boy" get ugly, when a table of battle-hardened soldiers wouldn't keep quiet. Jack Berry asked them once to be quiet but was greeted with an 'or what?' response from the soldiers. The beating that the whole group took at the hands of Jack Berry alone that night ended only when Howard pulled him out of the lounge before the police arrived. The Albion Hotel's owner Bill Touhey told the police he did not recognize the 'two boys' though who beat up the group of soldiers that night.

Street smart but only sixteen or seventeen in a rough post-war Ottawa, Howard Darwin learned when to 'call it a night' when out drinking at the Albion or elsewhere. Howard always left when the bigger and tougher friends that he was out with (like Jack Berry) were leaving, so that he wouldn't get 'jumped' on his way home later. In a 'just one more drink' scenario one Friday night around this time, a couple of Howard's friends implored him to go with them to Hull for a swing band that was playing in a bar over there. Howard declined to join them that night because he desperately wanted to get home for the Gillette Cavalcade of Sports radio show which was featuring a boxing telecast of a fight he wanted to hear live. Saturday morning arrived with the news that in a taxicab in Hull the night before; a knife was brandished, a cabbie was robbed - and two of Howard's friends were now in jail. Once again, boxing was there to save a young Howard Darwin from making bad choices.

As a sixteen-year-old apprentice watchmaker for Tim Burke in 1947, Howard Darwin was asked to deliver a repaired watch as arranged to a client who was having lunch at the prestigious, members-only Rideau Club on Wellington Street, directly across from Parliament. *"For longer than Confederation itself, the Rideau Club has been an influential part of the nation's capital and played an important role in Canada's national life."* [7] Howard was aware of the Rideau Club's 'all white' pedigree since 1865, as well as its refusal to grant membership to neither Jews nor women at the time. Howard got inside the front door with the repaired watch for Tim Burke's customer, but could never have imagined such opulence existed in Ottawa - let alone just a few blocks from his own Skid Row on Nicholas Street. It was a brief look however, because young Howard was promptly turned away and sent around back to the 'Tradesman's Entrance' or 'Kitchen Deliveries' door where he could leave his package. Howard Darwin vowed that he would someday be good enough to walk through the front door of the Rideau Club as a member – and he eventually did.

While learning his trade with Tim Burke, Howard Darwin also became something of a grandfather clock specialist which frequently brought him to Laurier House at 335 Laurier Avenue East. Laurier House was owned at the time by the Liberal Party of Canada. It was once the residence of former Prime Minister Sir Wilfred Laurier, and was the current residence of Prime Minister William Lyon Mackenzie King. Seventeen-year-old Howard would be summoned by Mackenzie King's staff to clean, lubricate and rebalance the many clocks in the big house, but in particular to remove any chimes or alarms from any new clocks received by the precise and superstitious Prime Minister. Mackenzie King didn't want any of the timepieces in the home to make noises. Howard Darwin often had the run of Laurier House once inside, after using the side entrance where a bored RCMP officer was stationed who simply waved to Howard on arrival. On one occasion Howard came around a corner upstairs and surprised Mackenzie King's little terrier who barked and snapped at the young apprentice. Howard kicked the sassy dog down the hall, and was never bothered by it again. Another time the Prime Minister himself stayed in the study and silently watched Howard while he fixed a clock; an encounter that Howard found 'creepy'.

Mahatma Gandhi was assassinated in India on January 30, 1948. Prime Minister Mackenzie King had been to India a few months prior and had met with Gandhi. In early February of 1948, Laurier House received an ornate, solid gold mantel clock as a gift from Gandhi which had been shipped to Canada prior to his assassination. Mackenzie King was 'spooked', and instructed his household staff not to touch the parcel that had just arrived from a 'dead man' in India, until his watchmaker (Howard Darwin), could get to Laurier House to unpack it, remove the chimes, and set it up on his mantel above a fireplace at Laurier House. Howard Darwin also maintained that he had carved his initials somewhere inside one of the Laurier House grandfather clocks on a staircase landing for his own posterity! (pg. 44)

After serving his jeweler's apprenticeship from age sixteen to age eighteen in 1946 and 1948 at Tim Burke Jewellers, and with his Watchmaker's trade papers now in hand, Howard Darwin moved out to Wellington Street West to work for Bruce Harvey at Stephen-Harvey Jewellers in the fall of 1948. Here Howard often clashed with owner Bruce Harvey however, and it reaffirmed his desire to run his own store (and make millions) someday.

(7) McCreery, Christopher: 'Savoir Faire, Savoir Vivre' (Rideau Club 1865 – 2015); pg. 1

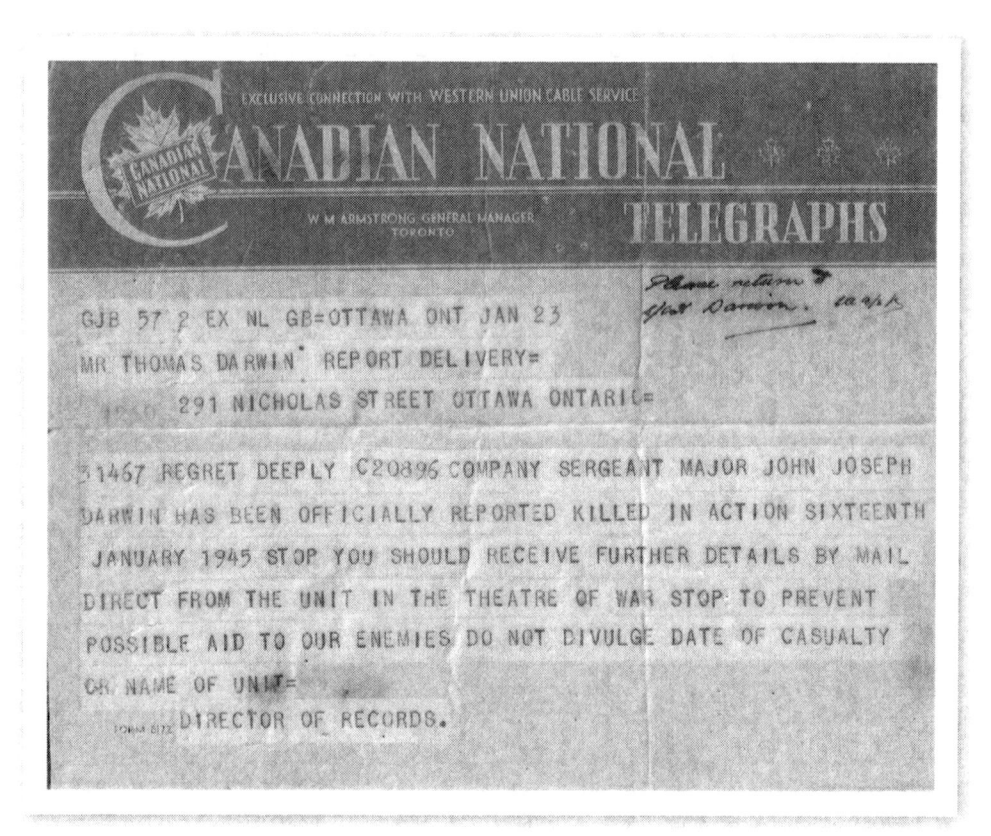

Picture IV1: "Jack"; John Joseph Darwin 1920-1945

VE Day in Ottawa

JEFF DARWIN

MANY WAIT TO ENTER COURTROOM AT OTTAWA MURDER TRIAL — A section of th[e la]rge crowd which began to gather an hour before the Stoneman murder trial resumed at 10.[30 th]is morning is shown in a corridor of the Carleton County courthouse. They were seeking ad[m]ission to the courtroom to hear the charge to the jury delivered by Mr. Justice Barlow, the pre[si]ding judge, before putting the fate of Eugene Larment, Wilfrid D'Amour and Albert Henderso[n]

Picture IV2: "I had a cold"; Howard Darwin pictured to the immediate left of the uniformed officer's cap on right/foreground

THE TEN COUNT

Post-war Ottawa: Albion Hotel; Charlie Lapointe, Percy Darwin, Eddie Lindsay; Howard with Friends; Streetscape; Rupert with Friends

Apprentice Watchmaker, Laurier House

V – SOMEONE IN HIS CORNER

On the westbound streetcar that made its way from Centretown up to Wellington Street West and Stephen - Harvey Jewellers each day in 1949, eighteen-year-old Howard Darwin could not help but notice the fair skinned beauty who usually rode the same car each morning to her job at nearby Patton's Cleaners. One day the stars finally aligned for Howard, and seventeen-year-old Connie Goudie sat down beside him. *"It's going to be a great fight"* Howard said, motioning towards the placard near the front of the car advertising the upcoming Gale Kerwin (Welterweight boxing) fight at the Auditorium. *"Have you ever been to the fights? Its only 25 cents."* With that smooth introduction Howard Darwin and Connie Goudie enjoyed their first date – a night at the fights. Always the gentleman as well as the businessman, Howard had sealed the deal for less than a dollar, including the two five-cent bus fares! It turned out to be the best investment Howard would ever make. (pg. 52)

Connie was living with her mother and brothers at the time in a subsidized veteran's apartment at 589 Rideau Street (the "Wallace House"). Connie Goudie was from a tough paper mill family and was raised on Broad Street in Lebreton Flats until the outbreak of World War II, where she had lived the same kind of poverty and had known the same kind of desperation as Howard Darwin had. Both had an abusive, alcoholic father – making them true, independent and kindred spirits. Whereas a real treat for a boy from Nicholas Street was to escape to the Ottawa Boys Club for a dime in annual dues, a young girl could escape "The Flats" for a whole day of swimming at the Plante Bath on Preston Street - followed by a hot shower with real soap – in exchange for a hard-earned nickel. (pg. 52) Connie herself was known on The Flats as the toddler who once survived being hit by a streetcar at the north end of Preston Street, with only a scrape on her head! They were both pretty tough kids.

With his new girlfriend living a full thirty minutes away on foot, or fifteen minutes plus an outrageous five-cents on a bus or streetcar, Howard Darwin knew that he was going to have to step up his dating game somehow if he was going to continue to impress young Connie Goudie; and now he had a plan. Howard's good friend Carl O'Leary had just acquired an unreliable old Ford for the reasonable price of $50 - complete with a rumble seat, faded paint and dented fenders - but what O'Leary didn't have was a wrist watch. So in the summer of 1949, eighteen-year-old Howard traded O'Leary his more reliable used watch in exchange for a 50% ownership in O'Leary's well-used Ford, and the courtship was on. Some of Howard and Connie's first dates with the car included Carl O'Leary too, while Howard was learning to drive and the boys were still fighting over use of their new shared transportation. When Howard and Connie did get out on their own though, Connie was usually relegated to push starting the stalled car because Howard would never relinquish the stick-shift which he maintained was 'very complicated for the uninitiated'. Connie Goudie remained unimpressed. (pg. 52)

The courtship was fast and furious, and just months after meeting her on the streetcar for the first time, Howard Darwin proposed to Connie Goudie on Connie's eighteenth birthday: July 10, 1949. To seal the deal, Howard had made an arrangement with the gemstone salesman that called on Stephen – Harvey Jewellers, and presented Connie with a large diamond solitaire set in white gold – the engagement ring that Connie Darwin wears to this day.

The newly engaged couple worked hard and saved money for their wedding, with the occasional weekend afternoon treat at Hogs Back for swimming or ice cream. Howard once rented a canoe at Dows Lake, and he and Rupert paddled it down the Rideau Canal to the pre-arranged meeting spot down the hill from the Old Man's rowhouse on Nicholas Street to meet his fiancé, Connie. There Rupert hopped out, but Howard failed to hold the canoe against the wall and railing of the canal while Connie was getting in and - with one foot on the wall and one in the drifting canoe - Connie ended up swimming in the stagnant, brown waters of the canal! Connie Goudie remained unimpressed. (pg. 53)

In July of 1950, Mackenzie King died just eighteen months after leaving office. Howard Darwin felt compelled to say farewell to his old customer, and joined the crowds who lined Wellington Street as Mackenzie King's body was driven to Union Station for one last train ride slowly past 291 Nicholas Street and out of Ottawa for the last time. In 1951, the City of Ottawa purchased the private Ahearn & Soper electric streetcar system from Thomas Ahearn and Warren Soper. Ahearn's private, local transportation system already boasted 130 streetcars and 61 buses at the time. Ottawa was growing up too.

In 1950, Howard Darwin was complaining so much about working at Stephen-Harvey Jewellers (over a beer at the Albion Hotel one night), that the hotel's sympathetic owner - Bill Touhey - offered Howard a rent-free arrangement on his unused and unkempt unit next door at 39 Nicholas Street. (pg. 56) The unit was three attached doors down from the Albion's lounge entrance, and was unused because it was slated to be torn down for an expansion of the hotel on the Nicholas Street side. With that early hand up, Howard Darwin got his wish to be his own boss again at the tender age of nineteen with The Watch Clinic, which he later renamed Darwin's Watch Clinic. Soon after this timely offer from Bill Touhey, Howard told his boss Bruce Harvey that he was leaving Stephen-Harvey Jewellers to open his own store. Bruce Harvey was quite unhappy and told Howard that 'you'll never make it on your own', and 'you'll be back in a month asking for your old job back!' Howard Darwin ran Darwin's Watch Clinic at 39 Nicholas Street on his own from 1950 to 1955, with only the occasional help (and unpaid labour) of his fiancé Connie Goudie. By 1953, Howard had parlayed his initial $647.15 in savings into a Darwin's

Watch Clinic's annual net profit for the store of $1,981.42 according to Roger Latendresse, CA. (pg. 56)

In the fall of 1951, twenty-one-year-old Howard Darwin was keeping a close eye on his seventeen-year-old brother Rupert to ensure that Rupert stayed off the streets and in school. Although he was not a disciple of the Sweet Science of boxing like his older brother Howard, Rupe was an athletic kid who excelled at most sports and in particular basketball. A couple of Rupe's fellow gym rats put Rupert up to asking the 'Proprietor of The Watch Clinic' if he might be able to sponsor them into a men's basketball league that winter. Not really having the disposable income to do much beyond helping his little brother Rupert alone, Howard did what he always did best – he hit the streets to hustle up a full team sponsorship including uniforms – with some strings attached. That winter, the local Pure Spring bottling plant had a new '7-Up' team in the league, including player/coach/manager/owner Howard Darwin, his good friend Earl "Smokey" Davis, and even his fiancé Connie's little brother, Gerry Goudie, in the lineup. So, Howard Darwin's first sports franchise then was neither hockey nor baseball; it was his reluctant 'ownership' of a men's amateur basketball team! (pg. 54)

By the summer of 1952 the Old Man moved Rupert and Howard to 229 Granville Street in Eastview where twenty-one-year-old Howard had to share a bed with his eighteen-year-old brother Rupert. Meanwhile Connie had moved herself with younger brother Gerry and her mother Irene to a more affordable rental home on Marquette Street in Eastview. The home was affordable because it wasn't quite finished yet – the bathroom was an outhouse in the back yard! (pg. 56) After just two months it was off to another rental flat at 439 Laurier Avenue for Connie and her family. It was clearly time for the long-engaged couple to improve their mutual housing situation - together.

Howard and Connie's nearly four year engagement was not without its issues. Connie maintains that her engagement ring was getting 'worn out' from being thrown back at Howard, and just before Christmas 1952, Connie Goudie broke off their engagement for the last time. On Valentine's Day 1953, Connie was out on a date with someone else, while Howard was back in the Goudie's kitchen at 439 Laurier

Avenue with flowers and chocolates for her mother Irene. When Connie arrived home that evening Howard was finally gone, however he had convinced Irene to plead his case with her daughter because 'Howard is just pining away without you'. Connie reluctantly agreed to give Howard one more chance, and Howard rushed over to see Father Connolly at St. Joseph's Church on Laurier Avenue. Howard was in a big hurry to close on this deal before Connie could change her mind, however Father Connolly refused to marry them until after Lent!

Howard Joseph Darwin (aged 22), and Constance Anne Goudie (21), were married the first Saturday following Lent on April 11, 1953. Due to the timing and their very modest means, attendants were chosen (at least in part) by who had suits or dresses that would match. Rupert Darwin was Howard's best man and Jackie Loftus was Connie's maid of honour. Connie's older sister June and her husband Bill Drinkwater had matching outfits so they were both attendants, as was Howard's older sister Josephine and Howard's friend Eddie Lindsay's older brother Jack, who also had a navy suit that fit him in the spring of 1953. (pg. 56) A small reception followed at June and Bill Drinkwater's house at 364 Lafontaine Street in Eastview, which was catered by a local bakery and restaurant owned by Cecil Morrison and Richard Lamothe (who earned great success later on as Morrison Lamothe Bakery).

For their honeymoon Howard was really going all out. Although his plans initially included bringing his younger brother Rupert, fiancé Connie said 'no way!' and Rupert was instead left in charge of Darwin's Watch Clinic for the week. With their honeymoon destination set for the Chateau Frontenac Hotel in Quebec City, Howard was now ready for his very first airplane ride there aboard Trans-Canada Air Lines. The return trip home was aboard the Canadian National Railway (Trans-Canada Airline's parent company), where the newlyweds spent the final weekend of their honeymoon with the Connellys at the Hotel Laurier in Montreal.

Howard and Connie's first matrimonial home was a one-room apartment in an old house at 97 Metcalfe Street. As a wedding present, Carl O'Leary built them a pull-up table with drop-down legs that was hinged to one wall, and a standup closet with a curtain front for their few clothes along another wall. It was very small, but they were together and without their surviving parents and siblings at last.

On one of their more memorable dates as newlyweds, Howard and Connie Darwin's good friend, Ottawa Rough Riders star running back Avatus Stone, took the couple to the Gatineau Club in October of 1953 to meet Bill Kenny and the famous Ink Spots band. Another favourite dance hall destination for young Howard and Connie was the Standish Hall over in Hull. (pg. 57) Avatus Stone was particularly fond of the newlyweds and socialized with them regularly, including the night Howard and Connie had to rescue Stone from Syracuse with a borrowed car. Avatus had snuck out of the Riders' training camp without permission to spend the evening with his girlfriend back in Syracuse - but hit a cow on his way back!

Over the winter of 1953-1954 Howard worked diligently in the Beaver Boxing Club gym with Jimmy Berry in preparation of taking Jimmy professional that spring in New York City. The Berry brothers (Jack and Jimmy) had been raised by their grandmother up on King Edward Avenue however, and now Jimmy Berry was the last one left to return the favour and watch over their grandmother. Despite a great amateur ring record and good professional potential, Jimmy "Irish" Berry reluctantly retired from boxing at the age of twenty-three to continue working in Ottawa and be closer to his aging grandmother. Howard Darwin would have to keep searching for his 'contender'.

On June 1, 1954, Howard Darwin staged a successful live, professional wrestling card featuring his idol, Joe Louis as a celebrity referee in the old Auditorium at 180 Argyle Avenue. (pg. 56) Joe Louis was always popular with the ladies wherever he went, but none admired the former world champion more than Howard! (pg. 56) Howard was getting rental breaks on the Auditorium for his promotions at the time from Auditorium owner and famed sports promoter Tommy Gorman, who had returned to Ottawa from the U.S. in 1945 to buy back the 7,500 seat indoor arena that he had originally built in 1923 with Frank Ahearn (who was the only son of Thomas Ahearn - Ottawa's original technology entrepreneur).

By September of 1954 the Ottawa Athletics professional baseball team which Howard had enjoyed taking either Rupert or Connie to the (affordable) ball games at Landsdowne Park in the early 1950s, packed up and headed to the U.S.. Howard (along with many other Ottawa baseball fans) was very disappointed. The Athletics had grown tired of battling their opponents on a very makeshift Landsdowne Park ball diamond, as well as Ottawa's vociferous mayor, Charlotte Whitton, at every turn. Howard would need to do something about that as well someday.

Mayor Whitton seemed opposed to all things sporting related and was particularly opposed to both beer sales in general and to games or commerce of any kind conducted on Sunday. Whitton was originally appointed as the first female mayor in North America in 1951 upon the death of the sitting mayor, Grenville Goodwin, and subsequently won mayoralty elections for Ottawa in 1952, 1954, 1960 and 1962. Howard Darwin and Charlotte Whitton never did see eye-to-eye, and would go on to have their own battles over the years.

When their sympathetic commercial landlord Bill Touhey found out that Connie was pregnant with her first child in the winter of 1955, Touhey felt that Connie needed to be a mother more than she need to help Howard at the jewellry store, and he gave them a 'pre-delivery' deadline to move out of the space that he had been planning to redevelop in any event. With that incentive and deadline, Howard secured rental space for a new jewellry shop in an existing shoe store on the ground floor of a large old house at 1308 Wellington Street, not far from where he used to work at Stephen-Harvey Jewellers (1208 Wellington Street), and where Connie used to work at Patton's Cleaners.

During the winter of 1954 and 1955, Howard was helping his old friend Carl O'Leary who was renovating 1308 Wellington for the new store, while a pregnant Connie managed Darwin's Watch Clinic – with no washroom – on her own. With the closest washroom at the Albion Hotel three doors down, poor Connie had to resort to a coffee can in the back when she (frequently) needed to pee! Eventually their friend Eddie Lindsay (younger brother of their wedding usher Jack Lindsay), was pressed into service each afternoon on his own way home from work to give Connie a welcome washroom break at the hotel, while Eddie minded Darwin's Watch Clinic for her!

Lebreton Flats, Connie Goudie, Plante Bath, First Car, Rideau Canal

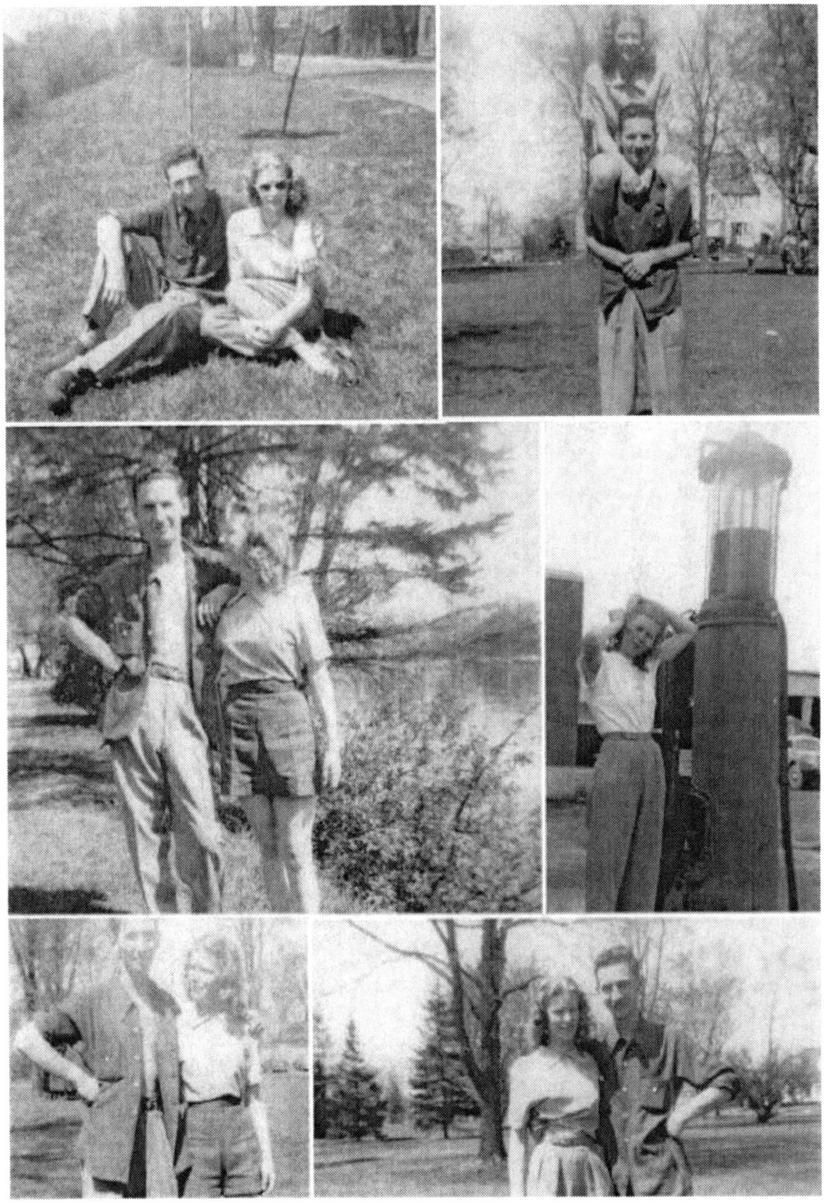

Picture VI: *"First Franchise 1951"* – Left to Right:

(standing:) Howard Darwin, Armand Villeneuve, Gerry Goudie, Gilbert Chouinard, Earl Davis, (sitting:) Jack Bowerman, Herbie Metrilla, Rupert Darwin

THE TEN COUNT

55

JEFF DARWIN

Picture V2: Howard and Connie at Standish Hall in Hull, Que.

VI – PUTTING DOWN ROOTS

The Grand Opening of Howard Darwin Jewellers at 1308 Wellington Street was on Saturday, April 16, 1955 with an eye-popping Grand Opening Special: mystery gift/grab bags for the first 1,000 customers at just $1 each! The grab bags were a big hit in the neighbourhood, but the real genius of the new 1308 Wellington Street location was the upstairs apartment that would eventually became the hot stove, boiler room and incubator offices required for Howard Darwin's future promotions and schemes – once he was able to find a way to buy the old building that is! Twenty-four-year-old Howard Darwin felt that the west end of the city was more ripe for development, and both he and Connie felt more comfortable starting their family away from their childhood hardships and poverty in downtown Ottawa. (pg. 68)

While the retail hours at Howard Darwin Jewellers were very long and hard on his whole family, Howard did fall into a comfortable routine of meeting and greeting his Wellington Street neighbours most days at places like Kelly Funeral Home (now Lauzon Music), Carver's Drugs (now Parma Ravioli), the CIBC (now Supply and Demand), Hilliary's Cleaners and Albert's Flowers (where Howard parked his car in the back yard and young Jeff Legault who lived above Albert's often washed it), and of course the kid Bobby Feller who lived with his folks above Howard's new jewellry store (now Watson's Pharmacy). Lunch for Howard in those days was often served by Dorothy Rheaume at the West End Bowling Lanes.

Howard was a living 'historian' of his hometown. Name a street corner anywhere in 50s or 60s Ottawa, and Howard could give you the four businesses on the corners and likely who owned them - or who might have started the business and then sold it. You wouldn't gain that kind of knowledge just driving the streets. Howard had earned his insights by walking them all at one time or another.

It was another year or two before they could afford to hire an employee to cut down on the sixteen hour days that Howard was putting in at the store at the time. In the early days Howard Darwin Jewellers was more of a 'bartering centre' by necessity, where Howard would trade his jewellry and giftware for virtually anything (besides food) that his young family might require. And despite leaving only the least expensive giftware and costume jewellry in the front windows each night, smash and grab break-ins were common at the store. Howard bemoaned having to respond to alarms in the middle of the night to clean up and arrange for the costly front showcase glass replacement every few months. (pg. 68)

Shortly after opening the new store in the summer of 1955, Howard and Connie Darwin moved from their 'one room' apartment to a larger, 'one bedroom' apartment on Clearview Avenue in time for the birth of their first child, Kim Mary Darwin; born on July 7, 1955. Kim Darwin was named after Hollywood starlet, Kim Novak, whom Howard had taken note of in Novak's 1954 breakout movie "Pushover".

In 1957 Howard, Connie and daughter Kim Darwin moved to a larger two bedroom apartment nearby on Lanark Street in time for the birth of their second child, Nancy Ann Darwin born on August 9, 1957. Howard's taste in music at the time had evolved from big bands to the more popular music from the "Rat Pack" and its patron (and huge fellow fight fan), Frank Sinatra. One of Sinatra's songs that Howard Darwin liked in particular was "Nancy With the Laughing Face", a song that Sinatra recorded earlier believing (wrongly) that it was written specifically for his daughter Nancy Sinatra who was four years old in 1957. So, Howard and Connie's second daughter Nancy Darwin was in effect named after Nancy Sinatra.

With more mouths to feed and little retail help now available from Connie who was busy raising their growing family, Howard's mind was kicking into overdrive thinking of new schemes to earn bigger money. It was around this time that Howard accepted the application of Joe Fagan to help him run Howard Darwin Jewellers. It was fortunate that there was no job description for the young Irishman Fagan, because he would become both the right and left hands of Howard Darwin for nearly forty-five years. (pg. 68)

This allowed Howard to put down his entrepreneurial roots on Wellington Street with the purchase of the whole building, where he was only renting up until that point at number 1308. Soon thereafter, Howard couldn't pass up the opportunity to purchase the old Brewer's Retail location next door on the west side of Howard Darwin Jewellers, and proudly announce from 1310 Wellington Street that he was now the "Trophy Centre of Canada's Capital". (pg. 68) Childhood friend and fellow Nicholas Street survivor, Eddie Lindsay, then joined the team at Howard Darwin Jewellers to keep up with the store's growing trophy and plaque engraving demand.

Although he was already a veteran Ring Rat and wrestling promoter by age twenty-seven, on March 17, 1958 Howard Darwin finally staged his first major fight card with his first major sports love: boxing. The headliners on Howard's ambitious first fight lineup at the Ottawa Auditorium that night were lightweights Davey "The Whip" Dupas from New Orleans (pg. 69), and local favourite Gale "Flash" Kerwin (who was now fighting out of Valley Stream, N.Y.). Howard had poured his meager life savings up to that point into the rent, advertising, travel expenses and purse guarantees for the professional fighters on this seminal St. Patrick's Day. Advance ticket sales were slow but when the big day arrived the walk up crowd backed up the ticket counters, and the first bouts had to be delayed while over 5,000 people crammed into the Auditorium to set an Ottawa live boxing attendance record that stands to this day.

Kerwin won the fight; the crowd went nuts; and Howard Darwin was hooked on live event promotion. From that night forward the local Watchmaker became a full time Sports Promoter, and his right hand man - Joe Fagan - was now effectively running Howard Darwin Jewellers without much supervision for the next thirty-seven years, in addition to managing Howard's box offices!

On August 22, 1958 Howard Darwin rented the Old Auditorium to introduce Ottawa fight fans to a new kind of boxing experience: closed circuit television. That night Ottawans strained to watch Floyd Patterson of Brooklyn, N.Y. defeat Roy Harris of Cut 'n Shoot, Texas half a world away in Los Angeles. The grainy black and white images projected on the giant screen were out of sync to the crackling audio of Don Dunphy calling every blow, but it was live and it was magical. Howard was only twenty-seven and had already made it into his own fight night heaven!

By this time Connie Darwin had seen their savings plowed back into events and commercial real estate too many times, and gave Howard an ultimatum to buy a first home of their own for their growing family. The young family of four soon moved into a newly constructed bungalow built by Bob Campeau on Tavistock Road in Queensway Terrace North early in 1959. The purchase price for Tavistock was twelve thousand dollars. Within one year, a friend at Campeau Construction convinced them that a larger home in Campeau's newer Queensway Terrace North sub-division would be a better place to raise their family. Connie sold the bungalow on Tavistock for an incredible sixteen thousand dollars and the Darwins were on the move again! When they made it over the Queensway to the new Campeau sub-division to the south, it was initially only as far as Sudbury Avenue while Malone Crescent was finished. Fortunately the young Darwin family was 'light' on possessions at the time and their final short move was made over countless trips by children's wagon – a throw-back to Howard's Newsboy origins!

In the spring of 1960 they moved into their second owned home: a modest, three-bedroom split-level house on Malone Crescent, and never moved out. The house cost an outrageous eighteen thousand, five hundred dollars. It was the last home they would ever need.

And right on cue, Connie gave birth to their third child on July 27, 1960 – and now they were five. There was never any question or discussion over whom Howard Darwin's first son would be named: John Joseph ("Jack") Darwin was the apple of his father's eye, and would naturally be named for the beloved older brother that Howard had lost in Holland during World War II.

Business for Howard Darwin was doing well in 1962-1963, while at home all that was left to complete Howard's family was a second son - the apple of his mother's eye this time. So, on Sunday, January 13, 1963 - while Howard took his first three kids out tobogganing - Connie gave birth to their final child. Connie and Howard's new baby was named Jeffrey Mark Darwin, after the popular Brooklyn-born actor Jeff Chandler. Howard scarcely had time to notice though; there was a big 'wrassling' show to put on at the Coliseum on Tuesday night after all! (pg. 69)

As much as Howard Darwin idolized the boxers growing up, he grew to love promoting the 'wrasslers' (as he pronounced it), when it came time to earn a living. Howard held Ontario Athletic Commission professional licenses for promoting both boxing and wrestling, and promoted over 300 different live and closed circuit sports events over the years - excluding the countless hockey and baseball games. The wrestlers however, never ever let him down and they were easily the athletes that Howard admired the most. The reason Howard maintained, was that 'wrasslers' always showed up; they never complained; and they worked the hardest for the very modest money that they earned in the pre WWF and WWE era. Lady wrestlers, midget wrestlers, animal wrestlers, tag teams, Faces, Heels, Tweeners, Jobbers or Tomato Cans – masked or unmasked – Howard appreciated how hard they all worked for him every time. (pg. 71)

Howard Darwin would regale mainstream athletes or sports writers for years with hilarious stories about colourful and often injured wrasslers that he had promoted. These wrasslers would usually drive all night through snowstorms and put on great shows for 100 or 10,000 fans – it didn't matter to them – wrestling fans (and promoters) always got their money's worth night after night. (pg. 71)

One retrospection piece written by Howard Darwin's personal friend and sports-writer confidant, Don Campbell, nicely summed up the craziness of promoting live wrestling in the 50s and 60s: *"And where he took the boxing seriously, he found fun in the wrasslers. Knew them well beyond just what they brought into the square circle. Darwin would promote in the afternoons in Ottawa, then at night in Cornwall. One favourite was the story about the wrestler who used to grapple with a bear. One night, with no place for the bear to stay, Darwin decided it could stay safely in the garage at his house in the west end, the one that he bought in the 1960s with three mortgages. The city eventually charged him for having a wild animal at his residence, but Darwin fought it and, with lawyer Peter Vice defending, the charge was thrown out without ever putting the bear on the witness stand."* [8]

And how Howard loved the wrasslers and all the trouble they could get into. In the 60s Howard always drove Chrysler Imperials, a big car of its time and when you're promoting three cards on a weekend, well the wrestlers had to get from Kingston to Ottawa and from Ottawa to Cornwall or wherever they were scheduled to fight. And Howard loved to drive and he had the biggest car and it beat paying someone else to drive wrestlers around. It was clearly entertaining for Howard Darwin too!

Perhaps Howard's best story is of driving down Highway 17 from Ottawa to Cornwall for an afternoon show at the old Water Street Arena. Howard was, naturally, the wheelman this particular day and he had Dr. Jerry Graham (Jerry Matthews) in his car with Sky Low Low, who was really Marcel Gauthier, a three-foot-six-inch, 86-pound midget wrassler out of Montreal, and Dick "Bulldog" Brower, only 5-8 but a powerful 280 pounds and more than a little crazy in his thinking.

Brower was known world-wide as a villain who could sell tickets and really get the fans engaged by screaming, yelling and throwing things at him. So down they go with Dr. Jerry Graham in the front and the Bulldog with Sky Low Low in the back, east towards Highway 138 and seemingly an uneventful trip; maybe an hour and twenty minutes at most. That was until they got about halfway there and Howard could hear one of the rear windows go down and the next thing he did was check his rear-view mirror to see Brower holding Sky Low Low completely out the window, Brower's hold as tenuous as the strength of the back of Sky Low Low's shirt. Howard managed to keep the car on the road but let out a yell to *"get the goddamn midget back in the car before he gets killed!*" For years afterwards, Howard would retell the story and couldn't help but having to interrupt himself with his laughter.

Then there was the time "Andre the Giant" (or Géant Ferré in France) - the "Eighth Wonder of the World" – headlined a big wrestling card in Ottawa for Howard, who then took him out for a late steak dinner after the event. Down they went to the Diamond Bar-B-Q on Bank Street where Howard just caught his friend and restaurant owner Saul Ages locking up for the night. Ages let the men in for a quick beer but explained that the kitchen was closed and the cooks were all gone.

"*Pas de problem – I'll cook,*" or something like that, said the 7-4, 520-pound Giant, who was really Andre Rene Roussimoff and said to be from the French Alps but was really from Grenoble. Then the Giant stood up and helped himself to four 'stubbies' (in *each* massive hand) from the bar as he showed himself into the kitchen where he fired up the grills and prepared a mountain of steaks and trimmings while Howard and Ages sat stunned out in the restaurant!

Apparently the Giant was really hungry and he knew his way around a kitchen. He just needed some food to go with the twenty or so cold beers he was enjoying while preparing their late dinner! Needless to say, the Giant didn't leave the steakhouse hungry and he even paid Saul Ages for the food he cooked himself.

There was a little more to the original wrestling bear story that remained untold publicly until now. "Terrible Ted", the seven-foot tall wrestling bear and his trainer were staying at Howard and Connie Darwin's suburban house on Malone Crescent on that first visit. After the sun had gone down and the Darwin children: Kim, Nancy, Jack and baby Jeff had been bathed and put in their pajamas for the night, Howard Darwin proudly assembled his young family on the quiet front steps of their new split level home for a surprise. The garage door was raised and the heavy steel cage on the trailer inside was opened, and out bounded a 600 pound black bear to 'do his business'. The bear was huge, smelly, loose and un-muzzled as he roamed freely, and peed and crapped on the freshly sodded lawns of the Darwin's neighbours for thirty minutes or so, returning to the Darwin's front lawn each time his trainer called him back.

The Darwin children were in fits of giggles and wide-eyed amazement, until being suddenly 'shushed' by Howard when a neighbour walking a small dog on a leash came around the corner of the darkened, gravel crescent (neither the streetlights nor the asphalt had been installed in the new neighbourhood yet). The little dog and the gigantic black bear both froze when they locked eyes on each other at the same time, but it took a few seconds for the little dog's owner to process what he thought he was seeing. When he was able to finally move, the terrified neighbour scooped up his dog and ran screaming back in the direction that he had come. Terrible Ted was quickly put back in his cage on the trailer in the Darwin's garage, and the laughing Darwin clan and their house guest scampered inside to chuckle about what their neighbour must be trying to convince his wife that he had just seen up on Malone Crescent! (pg. 72)

Whereas the spectacle of pro wrestling could only be experienced up close, professional boxing was often taking place in the major American centres, so Howard would promote those instead on his 'big screens' via closed circuit television around the province.

One time, Howard enlisted legendary Ottawa sports columnist Eddie MacCabe to oversee the 'action' up in Sudbury and Eddie was growing nervous as the start of the main event neared and technicians still couldn't get the long-distance feed. The Sudbury Arena was packed you understand, full of rough and rumble miners, and MacCabe feared the backlash if the fight didn't appear on the screen soon. A frantic MacCabe called Howard at his Civic Centre office to explain his concern. *"Eddie was yelling at me so I finally just hung up on him,"* recounted Darwin often. *"What the hell was I supposed to do from Ottawa? Fix the problem up there? The picture did finally show up and Sudbury got the fight and Eddie survived. We laughed a lot about that night."*

Being a real newshound and with a keen sense for historical events, it was not unusual for Howard Darwin to wake up his young family in the middle of the night for assembly in the den to watch man's first step on the moon on live television, or a breaking news report of a major assassination in the United States for example. Howard himself would hold court at the kitchen table until very late each night, watching television news casts on a small television on a shelf in the kitchen while reading newspapers from around the world. Kids who couldn't sleep and friends or reporters on deadline knew they could find Howard Darwin right there when needed. Because of it the Darwin kids all excelled at sports and current affairs, if little else, in school! It was not unusual for any of the Darwin teens to discover that their friends had been over to visit, but could never make it past a long visit with Howard in the kitchen when either coming or going from Malone Crescent.

There were many visitors to Howard Darwin's late night kitchen table ritual (and their refreshment choices never varied – always Labatt's 50 for Howard). There were however three regulars who may have set attendance records in the 70s. They were Father John Whelan (Sunday nights; always ginger ale), Alderman Claude Bennett (any night; coffee) and Detective Ken Spratt (most nights) who lived one block away on Sudbury Avenue and often stopped in when walking his dog – for a scotch!

(8) Campbell, Don: The Ottawa Citizen; pg. B7, Oct 23, 2009

JEFF DARWIN

Joe Fagan and Howard Darwin Jewellers

THE TEN COUNT

JEFF DARWIN

Dr. Jerry Graham, The Assassins, Sky Low Low and the midget wrestlers, Bulldog Brower, Whipper Billy Watson

Terrible Ted on Malone Crescent, Dr. Jerry Graham in the ring

VII – PIPED TELEVISION

While investigating ways to improve the poor closed-circuit television experience for his Auditorium and Coliseum sports fans in the early 60s – including the purchase of new 'colour' arena projectors – Howard Darwin was hearing from his U.S. sport promotion counterparts scheme just might work Howard thought. and friend Loren Cassina, that the next big thing could be 'pay' or 'piped' television. (pg. 79) Piped television would allow people to enjoy live sports from around the world from the comfort of their own homes. This scheme just might work Howard thought.

Piped television (wires from large community antennas run directly into homes to receive a few additional channels), had been recently introduced into a small number of homes in Hull and in Lynwood Village, so Howard took his chance and drafted an application to the City of Ottawa for the city's first full cable television license. The anti-visionary old mayor of the day, Charlotte Whitton, loudly and rudely dismissed Howard's application and the very idea outright, as a *"prostitution of the public system!"* [9], because Ottawa television set owners were already receiving the three, and sometimes four, local television stations free from their own 'rabbit ears' at the time. The City of Ottawa had no idea what to do with such a cheeky request from thirty-one-year-old Howard Darwin in 1962!

Having no luck with the City in this regard, Howard Darwin had his friend, Alderman Howard Henry, publicly embarrass Mayor Whitton at the Ottawa Hydro Electric Commission's annual general meeting in May of 1962. In a lively public exchange, forward thinking aldermen Howard Henry and James McAuley were slapped down by Mayor Whitton and the (patronage appointee) Commission Chairman, Stanley Lewis (who had been the 'steady hand' and former wartime Mayor of Ottawa). There would be no 'piped television' wires permitted on Ottawa Hydro's poles under Lewis and Whitton's watch!

Arena closed circuit television on the other hand, was not quite dead just yet. For his most lucrative closed circuit promotion ever, Howard Darwin had his wife Connie to thank in early 1964. The improbable closed circuit windfall came on the heels of Howard's money-losing heavyweight boxing event in February, when Sonny Liston gave up his title to Cassius Clay while sitting in his corner - staying on his stool. For this fight Howard had the closed circuit rights in North Bay, Cornwall, Ottawa and Jonquiere, but was required to rent the long distance telephone lines that brought the signals into these cities for a full thirty days from Bell Canada in any event. When he received the telephone pitch one evening at home in March of 1964, to have him *also* promote a closed circuit broadcast of a rock and roll concert by some band named "The Beatles" during his existing rental period, Howard Darwin said *"no thanks"*. Fortunately, Connie Darwin was within earshot of Howard's telephone offer and wisely interceded. Connie told Howard he should take the Beatles concert offer – they were a big deal now with the teenagers after all. Howard reluctantly took the concert offer, but only for his Ottawa and North Bay locations suggesting: *"It's the nuttiest thing I've ever heard of"*. [10]

An Ottawa newspaper described Howard Darwin's first closed circuit rock and roll concert this way:

"Absolute downright madness. There's no better way to describe the hysteria unleashed by 6,000 frenzied teenagers at the two closed circuit TV performances of the Beatles Saturday. The moment a robust young blonde came into view, shivering and shaking and singing out of the side of her large mouth, it was pandemonium. One shake of her shoulders, one flash of a camera, just any kind of action, brought forth a tumultuous roar. 'Make it

snappy,' complained a female Beatle bug beside me, but most seemed satisfied to wait. On came the Beach Boys, a quintet featuring the world's only adult boy soprano and an amazing leader who has convinced young America that it's possible to sing and chew gum simultaneously. A thousand fractured ear drums and one intermission later, on came the Beatles. The poor old Auditorium, soon to be demolished anyway, almost collapsed ahead of schedule. The rafters shook. Girls wept thankfully. Boys sniffled unashamedly. For 10 minutes nothing made sense. The roar grew, and grew, and grew. Then Beatle No. 1 approached the microphone. 'Thank you. Thank you very much. We'd like to play All My Lovin'. A man hammered my shoulder and gasped 'You a reporter? They're rolling on the floor down there.' I ran to the front and sure enough, a weeping, squealing girl was crawling, hypnotized, on her knees towards the giant screen. At least 20 girls had flopped out of their front row seats and were bouncing up and down on their knees. One portly lass pounded her head on the floor. Three girls, their eyes open wide, pressed their hands over their ears. Somehow this kept out the roars of the crowd and let in the harmony of their idols. Then horror of horrors, the screen went berserk in the middle of She Loves Me Yea Yea Yea. An angry catcall filled the hall for about five seconds. The picture improved but never perfected and the Beatles, up to 16 of them bouncing on the screen, carried on." [11]

In the Ottawa municipal elections held on December 7, 1964, Controller Don Reid defeated incumbent Mayor Charlotte Whitton, and the City of Ottawa was now set to mature and grow into a legitimate national capital. Under the leadership of Mayor Don Reid and new Alderman Claude Bennett, 1965 saw the rapid maturation of Ottawa as a city, starting with the municipal approval for Howard Darwin's exclusive cable television license for the west side of Bank Street, and Skyline Cablevision's exclusive cable television license for the east side of Bank Street by July, 1965. (pg. 80)

Howard Darwin realized that the cable television license for the western half of the City of Ottawa was way too large for him to handle on his own from both a technical knowledge and capital requirement perspective. Although still a little adverse to having business partners, Howard sought out several of the wealthiest and most respected local businessmen in Ottawa to be his new partners in the founding of Ottawa Cablevision Limited. These partners included retired farmer

Harry Leikin, esteemed lawyer Gordon Henderson and chartered accountant Roy O'Brien.

Harry Leikin was a favourite of Howard's in part because of the respect in which farmers throughout the Ottawa Valley held Leikin. A one-time cattle drover and owner of the Buckingham Dairy, Harry Leikin had travelled the region extensively yet rarely needed to buy a meal or stay at a hotel because farmers everywhere would insist that Leikin stay with them. Leikin had also brilliantly land-leased his farm on the south-east corner of Baseline and Woodroffe in Ottawa's west end for long-term commercial development. Howard was impressed.

When 'piped television' in Ottawa grew even faster than Howard Darwin had expected it to, Ottawa Cablevision Limited outgrew both its original technical office on Woodward Drive and its first administration office on Merivale Road. New consolidated space for the company was required and when some of his Cablevision partners showed reluctance to increase their investment in this Ottawa startup company, Howard called upon his new real estate business partner Earl Montagano once again and the pair purchased the former Garland & Mutchmore dry goods wholesalers building at 475 Richmond Road to lease back to Ottawa Cablevision Limited. (Earl had saved Howard financially on an earlier commercial real estate project.) Ottawa Cablevision Limited eventually purchased the 475 Richmond Road building and lands from Howard and Earl at a tidy personal profit for Howard and Earl.

In 1967, Toronto's Selkirk Communications purchased 49% of Ottawa Cablevision Limited, and in 1985, the Canadian Radio and Television Commission approved the sale of the remaining 51% to Selkirk. It was a great payday for the many local, original shareholders who had purchased their 12,816 shares apiece at just fifty cents each in 1967. One local shareholder whom Howard Darwin respected very much was reluctant to sell however. At one point during the selling process Harry Leikin pulled Howard aside and offered some sage advice: *"you sell only the fruit, not the tree"*. Misunderstanding Leikin initially, Howard replied that they may never see another offer like Selkirk's offer of $127 per share, to which the more senior Leikin clarified: *"then you and I should buy it instead"*. There was only one problem with Harry Leikin's wisdom however. Howard Darwin didn't have the $37 million it would take – but old Harry Leikin may have! The two Ottawa cable television companies on either side of Bank Street were both eventually acquired by Rogers Communications.

There were many more memorable Howard Darwin sports promotions held at both the Ottawa Auditorium at 180 Argyle Street and at the Coliseum building at Landsdowne Park. And then - in what Howard himself characterized as his 'most memorable promotion' - "Terrible Ted" came back to Ottawa on July 13, 1966. A retrospective piece written years later by Ottawa Sun columnist Pat MacAdam, sums up the bizarre Ottawa legal drama when Howard promoted an open challenge to Ottawa wrestling fans to wrestle the muzzled bear themselves for $3,000 in prize money:

"John Szigetti was a muscular 5-foot-8 Hungarian immigrant from Gatineau who worked as a welder. His truck had just been hit by lightning and it was uninsured. The $3,000. challenge purse would buy him a new one. Szigetti grappled with 'Ted', flung him to the mat and pinned him. The trainer refused to ante up $3,000 because he claimed the bear had not been pinned for 15 seconds. 'The Welder' sued Howard Darwin and what followed had to be one of Ottawa's most bizarre civil actions. Arthur Cogan acted for 'The Welder' and Jim Chadwick, now Mr. Justice James B. Chadwick, appeared for Howard and 'Terrible Ted'. The case was heard in the Supreme Court of Ontario before Mr. Justice Archibald Carter of Barrie and a six-man jury. The trial lasted three days. John Szigetti testified he put his arms around the bear, lifted him slightly off his feet to throw him off balance and then twisted him so that he fell on his back. He said he then fell on the bruin with his hands on the bear's neck and upper chest and pinned him for 15 seconds. He also testified his father was a butcher in his native Hungary and that he was accustomed to wrestling large pigs weighing several hundred pounds. Three witnesses who were paying spectators at the match testified that the bear had indeed been pinned but their estimates of time ranged from six to ten seconds. A curator from the National Museum brought a bear skeleton to court to augment his expert testimony. The Ontario Athletics Commissioner and sports reporters from CFRA and LeDroit were subpoenaed as witnesses. 'Tiger' Tasker, a wrestler and referee, testified that 'The Welder' tried to choke the bear. A veteran court employee quipped

that the trial should have been held under a big top with peanuts, cotton candy and soft drinks concessions. The jury deliberated for eight hours and 20 minutes before finding for Howard Darwin and 'Terrible Ted'. Joe Finn, The Citizen's legendary court reporter, wrote that it was the longest a jury was ever out in a civil action in Ottawa. When the jury came back at 11:40 p.m., Finn wrote that, in the courtroom, 'there was a cluster of newsmen, an assortment of wrestling fans and others (including a well-known Ottawa bookie)'. In dismissing the action, Mr. Justice Carter awarded costs to Howard. So, 'John the Welder' not only lost a truck, $3,000. and a court case; he also had to pony up court costs and Howard's legal fees. Two years later, Howard offered 'The Welder' a return match. He declined." [12]

(9) Brown, David: The Ottawa Journal, pg. 4, May 16, 1962
(10) MacCabe, Eddie: The Ottawa Journal, pg. 22, Mar 12, 1964
(11) Rupert, Bob: The Ottawa Citizen, pg. 13, Mar 16, 1964
(12) MacAdam, Pat: The Ottawa Sun; pg. 4, Dec 15, 2002

Ottawa Coliseum and Auditorium buildings

Ottawa Cablevision

VIII – MAJOR JUNIOR 'A' HOCKEY

In 1965, a small group of Ottawa sportsmen began talking about bringing the highest level of amateur hockey to the Nation's Capital in time for Canada's 100th anniversary in 1967. Ottawa's new Mayor, Don Reid, was also assembling another group of Ottawa sportsmen to establish the Greater Ottawa Sports Hall of Fame, and finally, all three levels of government were formulating their plans to redevelop Landsdowne Park with new football and indoor hockey stadiums as Ottawa's largest Centennial project. A thirty-five-year-old Howard Darwin was an exceptionally busy and integral part of all three of these groups by 1965.

With national Canadian Centennial plans well underway by 1966, Howard Darwin was still struggling as a promoter and labouring as a jeweler in Ottawa when a mutual friend put him in touch with Liberal Party of Canada rainmaker Keith Davey. Through this new federal Liberal connection Howard won a major national contract for his jewellry store to supply over 30,000 Canada Centennial Medals in four different styles. Some of the medals required different, decorative shields and some were personally engraved with the recipient's name. All the medals were manually attached to ribbons using a small ring and needle-nosed pliers. All of the ribbon and packaging work was carried out by the Darwin family plus friends and relatives on the rough-hewn, outdoor cedar picnic table *inside* the Darwin's modest dining room on Malone Crescent. The huge national contract was a major boost to the fortunes of the family and finally allowed Connie Darwin to purchase some new furniture for her home - including a real dining room suite!

Also in 1966, Howard Darwin was leading a group of Ottawa businessmen in an attempt to win an Ontario Hockey League Major Junior 'A' expansion franchise for the new Ottawa Civic Centre being built at Landsdowne Park. Howard's group was competing against several other Ontario cities, and was also competing in Ottawa against two other local groups led by Ottawa Rough Rider president Sam Berger, and radio station CFRA general manager Terry Kielty. All three Ottawa groups were being supported by Mayor Don Reid and Alderman Claude Bennett, who was also chairman of the city's Recreation and Parks Committee at the time.

By January of 1967, the Greater Ottawa Sports Hall of Fame project was launched by Mayor Don Reid. The Hall of Fame was the brainchild of Ernie Calcutt, chairman of the sports section of Ottawa's Special Centennial Projects Committee and the initial Board of Trustees was comprised of Howard Darwin, Alan Butterworth, Bill Westwick, Bill Touhey, Al Merrikin and Donat Vien. Thirty-seven former athletic greats from Ottawa formed the initial induction and their plaques and bios would eventually be placed in showcases along the north side concourse of the yet to be completed Ottawa Civic Centre arena. The Hall of Fame finally opened to the public in April of 1968.

On Wednesday, February 15, 1967 – some 14 years after the disappearance of major junior hockey in Ottawa – Howard was hobbling around on a painful broken foot that he would soon forget about, because the Ontario Hockey League finally announced that he had WON: *"Howard Darwin, 35, the sports promoter who is prepared to sponsor just about any action, has officially been named as winner of the Ottawa franchise in the OHA."* [13]

Howard Darwin's group - known initially as the Ottawa Bytown Hockey Club - was comprised of personal friends Bill Touhey, Bill Cowley (both ex-NHL stars), and Ottawa Alderman Howard Henry. The group managed to scrape together the outrageous sum of $30,000 for the Ontario Hockey League expansion franchise that would bring the league up to ten teams for the 1967-1968 season (Bill Touhey later sold his initial quarter-share of the Ottawa hockey club to Jack Kinsella). Howard Darwin did not even have the $7,500 initial investment, so Bill Touhey graciously lent Howard $5,000 and the group declared the thirty-six-year-old Darwin 'Club President'.

By mid-April of 1967, Howard Darwin held a press conference at the Sampan Restaurant to announce that he had lured seasoned Niagara Falls Flyers assistant coach Bill Long to Ottawa to build their new junior team from the ground up. Soon thereafter however, Howard was unable to obtain permission from the Gorman Family to use Howard's preferred team nickname - the "Senators" - so he settled on the "67's" in recognition of Canada's Centennial Year of formation. When asked by Ottawa Citizen columnist Bob Mellor about how the team name might look 'next year', Howard Darwin reportedly replied *"The San Francisco 49'ers have done alright with their name."*

In yet another business venture in the spring of 1967, Howard Darwin had learned from his contacts at the City of Ottawa about newly proposed municipal by-laws coming into effect the following year whereby parking spaces would need to be created for the employees and customers of any new commercial development. Howard moved quickly that year to purchase the used car lot at 1306 Wellington Street at the corner of Warren Avenue, immediately to the east of his Howard Darwin Jewellers store. With the dream of becoming a major commercial landlord, Howard obtained a 'pre-parking by-law' building permit on a rush basis from the city, and then hustled up a long-term lease with the Metropolitan Life Insurance company. Metropolitan Life signed for the first three floors of the building and construction was immediately started on Howard's new five-story office building with no new parking for either employees or customers.

Howard was pretty comfortable with approaching his banker with 60% of his office space pre-leased in 1968, but soon learned that the banks wouldn't touch the novice developer with almost no equity into his new building that was already under construction. Once again, Howard Darwin had over-extended himself and had neither money nor financing to complete his first commercial real estate project. The thought of selling their new home was out of the question as far as Connie Darwin was concerned (and there was virtually no equity in their first home at that point in any event), so Connie made the profound suggestion of contacting Howard's teenaged acquaintance, Earl Montagano, whom she heard was doing well in the heating and air conditioning business. Howard Darwin and Earl Montagano agreed to terms and quickly formed Darmont Holdings Ltd to complete the building. Howard was saved financially by Earl, and a new lifelong business partnership was formed. By the time that the Darmont Building at 1306 Wellington Street was completed, the new real estate partners had leased the final top two floors to the federal government for the secret, long-term storage for some of Canada's most valuable paintings before our National Gallery was built in 1988. There were even priceless sculptures stored in the basement – the Darmont Building was fully leased!

With the new Civic Centre arena still under construction the inaugural Ottawa 67's team opened their 1967-1968 season on the road and were forced to play their first home games at the Hull Arena. Led by their first team captain - Bill Clement of Buckingham, Quebec - the first hockey game ever played at the new Ottawa Civic Centre finally took place on Friday, December 29, 1967: *"More than 9,000 fans jammed into the Civic Centre not quite ready for the crush. Most of the building's 9,355 seats were in place but about 600 weren't. And tickets for those seats had already been sold. Fans had the option of getting their money refunded and six did just that. Most of the remaining 594 poured into the Coliseum to grab a chair for the night."* [14]

Following the Ottawa 67's inaugural season of futility in 1967-1968 (45 losses, 6 wins and 3 ties for just 15 points - last place in the 10 team OHL and easily the worst junior hockey team in Canada), the team and its young players settled down to earn a playoff position in just their second season of existence. Not coincidently, the Ottawa 67s were joined full-time in 1968-1969 (their second season) by a fourteen-year-old bantam-aged player from the Overbrook neighbourhood of Ottawa's east end named Denis Potvin in his first complete season as a junior. Denis Potvin was easily Howard Darwin's favourite of the many hundreds of hockey players that played for him in both Ottawa and London over the years. Howard and Denis' personal bond was forged through the early respect Howard showed to both Denis' father Armand, and to his older brother Jean Potvin who was an original Ottawa 67's defenceman in season one.

Remarkably, Denis Potvin was only thirteen-years-old when he first met the thirty-seven-year-old Howard Darwin when Potvin was called up by the Ottawa 67's to play the first of just three games in that inaugural season. It sounded like this: *"Denis Potvin, who'd been playing for a team in Alta Vista, raced down to the Civic Centre, and that night he made his rookie debut for the Ottawa 67's against Niagara Falls. He was 13 years old. Thirteen. And 5-8 and 185 pounds of menace and muscle. This boy, this 13-year-old boy, was playing with and against players six and seven years older but, even then, few were better, and even fewer were more physical or tougher with their fists. Those who saw it still talk of the time when he challenged to a fist fight the player who was to become the most fearsome goon in the NHL – Dave Schultz. Schultz was with the Richmond Robins and in an exhibition game, kept threatening Potvin, goading him to fight, until, finally, Potvin dropped his gloves, turned on Schultz and screamed, 'All right, let's go.' Schultz suddenly saw, or sensed, something that told him it would not be good for his health; he backed off, he chickened out. Dave Schultz was 18 years old. Denis Potvin, 13."* [15]

"Denis," says Howard Darwin, *"was given a very wide berth once his reputation was established. He didn't go looking for fights, but, by God, could he finish them. He was so competitive. I've never seen such great desire, and his anticipation and timing were unbelievable. He was a great hockey player. But, as tough as Denis was and despite the reputation he has of being the toughest of all 67's, I still think that honor goes to his brother, Jean. He didn't go around looking to fight either, and it's a good thing. One time, two motorcycle guys, Hell's Angles, bashed into the back of his (Jean's) Volkswagen Beetle he'd just bought and fixed up. Then one of them began putting his boots to the car. Jean got out and kicked the living shit out of both of them. I mean, it was brutal. He left them lying on the road, and when the cops arrived, he was kicking the spokes out of their bikes. Jean used to protect Denis in the early days on the team until he realized Denis didn't need any."* [15]

While Jean Potvin was being unnecessarily protective of his kid brother Denis on the ice, Connie Darwin took matters a step further for the teenager when she visited Denis in the Riverside hospital in May of 1969. Denis' nose had been broken in a hockey fight that year and Howard had arranged for it to be reamed and reset at the end of the season. In typical fashion Howard was in Toronto at the time, so Connie took a large fruit basket and all four of her children in to see Denis Potvin in the hospital. The scene in the hospital room confused Connie a little but delighted the children - because the fifteen-year-old, heavily muscled, Denis Potvin was propped up in his bed with a bandaged face reading comic books!

In August of 1968, in what was the biggest bankruptcy sale in Canada at that time, a thirty-seven-year-old Howard Darwin, Central Ward Alderman and Central Canada Exhibition Association Director, Claude Bennett (aged 31), and local restauranteur Saul Ages (51) - all residents of Ottawa - purchased the London Nationals Major Junior A hockey team in the Ontario Hockey League and their home arena, the London Gardens, from Atlantic Finance for $500,000. At 5,700 seats, the London Gardens was the second largest privately owned arena in Ontario, behind only Maple Leaf Gardens at that time. The new Ottawa owners rebranded the team as the London Knights.

The plan for the 1968-1969 season in London was for Howard to run the hockey operations and promotions, Claude Bennett would oversee property development and maintenance, and the senior statesman of the ownership group - Saul Ages - would manage all financial aspects. Howard's younger brother Rupert Darwin was subsequently hired away from Quebec Hydro to move to London to run the arena concessions and to become the group's full-time eyes and ears in southern Ontario. Howard felt that the price was right, and told the Ottawa Citizen that *"We couldn't be happier, we feel we made a wise investment."* Tragically, partner Saul Ages (Diamond BBQ and other restaurants in Ottawa) passed away shortly thereafter and then Claude Bennett won a seat in the Provincial Legislature in 1971, so Bennett's shares in London passed into a blind trust controlled by Howard Darwin alone.

The resulting workload on Howard Darwin in the 70s was extreme. Howard would frequently make the six to seven hour drive (depending on traffic) to London to sign papers (or to fire his General Manager Doug Pratt for secretly trading Mark Howe's rights over Howard's objections!), then climb back into his car at days end to make the return trip home to Ottawa on the same day. Howard became a Highway 401 Road Warrior and was once involved in a large pile-up that totaled his Chrysler Lebaron, and injured several others that night. Howard actually enjoyed highway driving, usually on cruise control and sometimes sitting shoeless and cross-legged for comfort, listening to eight track or cassette tapes of big band leaders like Louis Armstrong. Howard Darwin never wore his seatbelt and the eventual advent of air bags was small comfort to his family in later years!

On one occasion, a call from Rupert about non-hockey staff concerns in London prompted Howard to make a mad dash there to meet with a union organizer and long-time staff members; General Manager Helen Jenner, 'the Popcorn Lady' Anita Wright, and several other non-hockey arena staff. The London union organizer asked Howard Darwin if he could stay in the meeting while the staff outlined their concerns to ownership. Howard said *"sure"*, and then asked if he might open the meeting then, which was agreed to by all present. Howard proceeded to pass out individual severance cheques with accrued vacation to every one of the London Gardens employees - including his own brother Rupert - which he and Rupert had calculated, written up and signed just prior to the meeting. The stunned employees looked at their cheques and asked their (protesting!) union organizer to step outside the room. Once the employees had ascertained that Howard was completely serious, they each in turn tore their own severance cheque in half, and returned the pieces to the table in front of Howard Darwin and never again raised the idea of forming a union at the London Gardens.

In June of 1971, Howard Darwin along with Ottawa real estate partners Earl Montagano and Roy O'Brien, purchased the commercial properties adjacent to the London Gardens that were known as The Treasure Island Shopping Centre for $1.4 million (the purchase from the Leon brothers of Toronto was widely reported incorrectly as $2.5 million at the time). The parcel included a large Metropolitan department store, a Leon's furniture store and twelve acres of parking.

Howard and his partners eventually sold the Treasure Island Shopping Centre in London, Ontario for $2.7 million in April of 1979.

On Friday, March 31, 1972 in Ottawa, a playoff game between the Ottawa 67's and the London Knights (both teams were owned by Howard Darwin at the time) became known as the 'Good Friday Bloodbath'; one of the ugliest, most infamous games in major junior hockey history. On this horrible night for owner Howard Darwin, who was vacationing in the Bahamas with his family, a post-game bench-clearing brawl involving both of Howard's hockey teams descended into complete chaos with hundreds of Ottawa fans – including 67's co-owner Howard Henry - jumping into the on-ice fray. It ended only when one hundred Ottawa Police officers converged on the Ottawa Civic Centre and at least fifty officers were required to escort the London Knight's bus to the Ottawa airport. The players on the bus packed the windows with their equipment bags for protection before the bus pulled out of the Civic Centre's underground. They were followed to the Ottawa airport by dozens of angry Ottawa fans in their cars!

The harrowing escape from Ottawa didn't end there for the London Knights: *"On the flight home, the Knights aircraft guided a small plane to a safe landing after it lost radio contact with all airports. A second small aircraft crashed killing four persons. The Knights' (chartered) DC-3 circled for 45 minutes searching for the planes during a snowstorm."* [16]

Although the Ontario Hockey League's Commissioner Clarence "Tubby" Schmalz deemed London responsible for touching off the riot, both coaches were fined, players from both teams were suspended, others were hospitalized, and London defenceman Dave Hutchison was charged by Ottawa police with assault causing bodily harm.

In a different London Knights franchise highlight on December 19, 1972, Coach Bill Long - with the help of some Junior A all-stars including Blake Dunlop and Denis Potvin from the Ottawa 67's - defeated the Moscow Selects 6 – 3 at the London Gardens. This was essentially the same Russian team that had just played Paul Henderson and the NHL all-stars in the famous 1972 Summit Series.

Memorable London Knights players from the time of Howard Darwin and Claude Bennett's ownership included Darryl Sitler,

Rob Ramage, Brad Marsh, Dino Ciccarelli, Dennis Maruk, Brendan Shanahan and Reggie Thomas.

By the spring of 1974 in Ottawa, the 67's President Howard Darwin was having disagreements with his partners Jack Kinsella, Bill Cowley and Howard Henry over the hockey operations and had to accept Coach Leo Boivin's resignation. Boivin's replacement would be a local minor hockey league coach, restaurateur and former Los Angeles Kings player, Brian Kilrea. Kilrea had caught Howard's eye through his recent success at out-coaching a touring Russian minor hockey team in a local hockey tournament. Thus began the very successful Brian Kilrea era which included the Ottawa 67's first Memorial Cup appearance in Vancouver in 1977, as well as their first Memorial Cup win in 1984 in Kitchener. Kilrea was joined initially by Gord Hamilton and later Bert O'Brien as coaching assistants. With Brian Kilrea at the helm, the Ottawa 67's rarely missed the playoffs and Kilrea went on to become Canadian major junior hockey's all-time coach with the most wins, and earn himself entry into the Hockey Hall of Fame.

Through the winter of 1979, Howard Darwin owned a jewellry store and an office building, ran two major junior 'A' hockey clubs in different cities, and was additionally the executive chairman of the OHA as well as the league's acting commissioner. Still, Howard's family were shocked when their slim and energetic forty-eight-year-old patriarch suffered a heart attack at home on March 14, 1979 following a family dinner. After assuming his customary position at the kitchen table reading newspapers after the others had gone to bed that evening, Howard had trouble moving his arms. Early the next morning daughter Nancy awoke to find her sleepless father at the kitchen table with empty Coke cans lined up that had been used to treat his self-diagnosed indigestion! When Nancy insisted on taking her father to the hospital, he in turn suggested that they by-pass the new west end Queensway Carleton Hospital in favour of the Ottawa Heart Institute. Obviously Howard knew more about what was happening than he would let on to his daughter. While recovering in the hospital he was caught locked in the washroom enjoying a last cigarette and a Kardish Delicatessen smoked meat sandwich!

In late January of 1974, a government courier delivered a package to Howard Darwin Jewellers on Wellington Street. In it was a letter from The House of Commons that read: *"Dear Howard. Thank you again for your kindness in sending me tickets to the Ali-Frasier event at the Civic Centre Monday night. It was a classic match and one that I would have been disappointed to miss. It is always a pleasure to chat with you and Mrs. Darwin who appeared to enjoy the contest as much as you and your sons. I have enclosed a photograph and copy of the Bill of Rights for Jack and Jeff. They are fine boys and can be justifiably proud of their father's notable contribution to sports in Ottawa. With all good wishes and kindest personal regards, I am, Yours sincerely, John Diefenbaker."* [17]

John Diefenbaker was a very passionate and knowledgeable fight fan. Like Howard Darwin, Diefenbaker loved the Sweet Science, and while in Ottawa from 1940 to 1978, as either the Prime Minister and 'in office' or in opposition, Howard always provided John Diefenbaker with a pair of the best tickets to every live or closed circuit boxing event that he promoted. Leading up to any major fight anywhere in the world, Howard's phone would ring and Minister Diefenbaker would say: *"Howard…its John…John Diefenbaker. How do you think the (upcoming) fight is going to go?"* One year for Diefenbaker's birthday, Howard sent his boxing friend a leather bound copy of the latest edition of Nat Fleischer's "Ring Record Book" (the Bible of Boxing). Within a few days, Diefenbaker called and said: *"Howard, you tell that friend of yours – Fleischer - that Tommy Burns was born Noah Brusso in Hanover, Ontario, and that he was not of French-descent, he was German, and I know that because my father taught him in school in Berlin, Ontario, which is now called Kitchener."*

In a 'total-site' rental of Howard Darwin's 5,075 seat London Gardens arena, American evangelist Kathryn Kuhlman brought her controversial 'Power of God Crusade' to London on June 18, 1974. The Kathryn Kuhlman Foundation's arena rental agreement was explicit: there was to be no food and beverage concessions available to the more than 8,000 faithful who would pack the day-long event from a catchment area of over 500 miles away. Howard had heard that this was done elsewhere to increase the Foundation's cash intake from the collection plates being passed through the crowds. Howard and his London Gardens concessions manager, younger brother Rupert Darwin, were one step ahead of Kathryn Kuhlman that day. The brothers temporarily rented, filled and installed over 100 extra pop and food vending machines along the concourse of the building to feed the huge crowds and increase their own 'take' from the event!

At the start of the 1975 hockey season, Howard Darwin bought out his Ottawa 67's partners Jack Kinsella, Bill Cowley and Howard Henry and immediately sold a 51% interest to his real estate partner Earl Montagano so that he could continue as a two-club boss with 49% of the Ottawa 67's and 66% of the London Knights in the Ontario Hockey League. It was Brian Kilrea's second season as the Coach and General Manager in Ottawa, and Howard was now firmly back in control.

Other memorable Ottawa 67's alumni from the Howard Darwin ownership era included Gary Roberts, Mike Peca, Darren Pang, Peter Lee and Shean Donovan. From his first Memorial Cup team, Howard always spoke fondly of Bobby Smith, Doug Wilson and Ed Hospodar. Despite being one of the most feared enforcers in hockey, Ed Hospodar was another of Howard's favourites for his gentle mannerisms and maturity off the ice. At the 1977 Memorial Cup tournament in Vancouver, Hospodar even drew an unusual roommate assignment in Howard's fourteen-year-old son!

In a November 1975 game in London between the Knights and the St. Catherine Fincups, several Fincups players climbed into the stands to fight the London fans in a scene reminiscent of the 1977 Paul Newman movie "Slapshot". The Ottawa Citizen followed up on the story this way: *"London Gardens owner and operator Howard Darwin was found guilty by the league of not providing adequate police protection. He was to be fined $250 and forced to post a bond of $5,000. 'There were 17 security guards in the place,' Darwin said, 'and the kid in the penalty box had to jump over the glass to go after the spectator. Any number of guards wouldn't have stopped that.' In conclusion, he told the league to go to hell. He would not pay the fine, or post a bond, and would not have played the next game. On the evening prior to it, the league rescinded the ruling, probably because they couldn't enforce it, and not because of any change of mind."* [18]

With their family now complete and hockey in particular in full swing, Connie Darwin was naturally pressing Howard for a family summer vacation of some sort. For their first attempt, Howard purchased a run-down cottage on Patterson Lake in remote west Quebec. After a substantial move-in ordeal with young children and a summers worth of provisions, Howard surprised Connie by heading back to Ottawa on business leaving her with four kids and no car! Connie sold the cottage after that first summer. On their second attempt Howard rented a cottage for the family in Grand Bend, but once again left Connie alone with the kids while he went to work in London to relieve the London Gardens management staff, so that they could have a summer vacation too. The Grand Bend experience wasn't repeated either. On his third attempt at a true family summer vacation Howard struck upon a winner for everyone that would become his family's annual August ritual: the all-inclusive Gray Rocks Resort in Quebec's Laurentian Mountains. Gray Rocks presented no additional cooking or cleaning work for Connie and was close enough to Ottawa for Howard to make (an infrequent) escape home for work. Howard rarely left a Gray Rocks vacation early though because he came to enjoy its great food, beach vibe and leisurely pace. The Darwin kids loved Gray Rocks too! (pg. 95)

(13) Koffman, Jack: The Ottawa Citizen; pg. 26, Feb 16, 1967
(14) Scanlan, Wayne: The Ottawa Citizen; pg. C1, Dec 29, 1987
(15) McRae, Earl: The Ottawa Sun; pg. 39, Feb 17, 1991
*(16) **Herbert**, John: The London Free Press; pg. 20, Feb 12, 1976*
(17) Diefenbaker, The RT. Hon. John G.: Personal Letter, Jan 30, 1974
(18) Mellor, Bob: The Ottawa Citizen; pg. 27, Nov 27, 1975

*November 1967: Howard Darwin and Bill Long
presenting Prime Minister Lester Pearson with a seating
chart and season's tickets to the Ottawa 67's*

The Original Ottawa 67's (1967–1968)

Ottawa 67's and London Gardens (lower right)

London Knights, Ottawa 67's team van, Darwin family at Gray Rocks

VIX – NO CONTEST: LOUIS VS. NELSON

In 1978, Beaver Boxing Club founder and most senior trainer Joey Sandulo called his friend Howard Darwin to tell him that there was a new kid at the gym that Howard should see. Howard – like everyone else who saw the new kid – was impressed with the incredible physique and fitness of the six-foot-four-inch Jamaican-Canadian heavyweight. At nineteen years old, Conroy Nelson was a specimen.

Howard asked: *"Why is all his weight on his back foot?"* Joey: *"He's a kick-boxer"* Howard: *"Well whatever the hell that is, get him to stop it before he ends up on his ass!"* Joey: *"Are you going to manage him then?"* Howard: *"Are you going to teach him how to fight?"* Howard Darwin and Joey Sandulo turned Conroy Nelson professional on November 20, 1978 at the Knights of Columbus Hall in Buckingham, Quebec: a TKO against American journeyman Sylvester Wilder. Howard was excited and felt that he had finally found his 'contender'. Instead, Howard's heavyweight nightmare had just begun. (pg. 104 with Gerry Cooney)

Howard and Joey slowly (and expensively) brought Conroy up through the ranks against progressively more experienced opponents. By 1981, Howard had Conroy Nelson ranked as the number one contender for the Canadian and British Commonwealth heavyweight titles that were both held at that time by a fellow Jamaican-Canadian fighter named Trevor Berbick of Halifax. Howard was trying to set up the title challenge for Nelson, and had traveled to Las Vegas with Connie for Berbick's April 11, 1981 loss to Larry Holmes. (Although it was the last time that Larry Holmes and Trevor Berbick would meet in the ring, it wasn't the last time the two would fight. Holmes would beat Berbick one more time in a bizarre street fight in Hollywood, Florida ten years later!)

At ringside in April of 1981 Howard got the chance to reconnect with his boxing idol Joe Louis who was working from a wheelchair as a Las Vegas casino greeter. Howard had heard that Louis was broke and in poor health, but was completely surprised and unsettled by how unwell Louis looked that night. The two old friends briefly reminisced about Ottawa and Joe Louis brightened up about that 'chicken liver place' (the old Town and Country Restaurant on Richmond Road). (pg. 106) The next day Connie and Howard were in a cab heading to the airport to return home to Ottawa when a news bulletin came on the radio saying that Joe Louis had died that morning. It was a very sad flight home for Howard. Howard learned later that Frank Sinatra, a huge fight fan himself, had quietly paid the funeral and burial expenses for the great Brown Bomber. (pg. 105)

Against the backdrop of the loss of his sporting idol, Howard set about to see how far he could take Conroy Nelson in the square circle: *"Darwin and Sandulo saw a champion in Nelson after he beat Leroy Caldwell of Las Vegas in a 10-rounder Nov. 12, 1980. Trevor Berbick had managed only a draw against Caldwell. So on July 21, 1981, Darwin's hopes were sky high when Nelson and Berbick met in Halifax for the combined Commonwealth and Canadian heavyweight title. The scales couldn't have been more heavily tipped in Conroy's favour. Berbick was out of shape. He was in the midst of a legal battle with his lawyer. Nelson was fresh from a training camp in White Plains, N.Y. where he had sparred 75 rounds with the likes of Leon Spinks and Renaldo Snipes, on Howard's dime, of course. Even if he did take four-mile cab rides to dinner each night to see a certain waitress, Conroy was in scary condition. The fight was a big deal in Halifax. Berbick and Nelson were in demand. They presented a winner's wreath at a featured horse race. Conroy looked super on the TV cameras. 'Everything was going great until they got into the ring and touched gloves,' says Sandulo. 'Conroy came back into the corner and he couldn't move. He* was like a zombie. Even if he had just run around the ring, Berbick couldn't have stayed with him.' The fight was stopped at 2:49 of the second round. Four years later, Conroy would last as long with a 19-year-old named Mike Tyson. By then, Howard Darwin had given up, fed up... Conroy Nelson autographed bad cheques like they were souvenirs. Long after Howard Darwin washed his hands of him, Conroy was sentenced to six months in jail for peddling cocaine. Conroy Nelson is the only reason Howard Darwin's middle name is not 'Midas Touch'." [19]

By the time Conroy Nelson resurfaced for his next fight in May of 1982 Howard Darwin was not actively representing Nelson and - in an effort to slow down the number of calls Howard was getting from collection agencies and law enforcement regarding Conroy's whereabouts – Howard finally sold Nelson's contract to Robert Goff and Robert Mudd of Cameron, Louisiana for $4,000 USD in March of 1983. Howard ran to the bank to cash their cheque before the new managers could change their minds!

For every Conroy Nelson that he encountered in boxing though, Howard would be quick to tell you about others in the sport like Joe Louis, Joey Sandulo, Shawn O'Sullivan or Ian Clyde – good, real people.

Greg Gayle was another of boxing's good people and a great kid. Gayle was a Canadian amateur lightweight champion with 77 wins and 15 losses in 1986 when the twenty-four-year-old fighter spurned other professional managers and trainers and instead asked Joey Sandulo and Howard Darwin to take him pro. (pg. 104)

Trevor Berbick's very next fight on the other hand turned out to be Muhammad Ali's *last* fight on December 11, 1981. Berbick continued to fight and was murdered in Jamaica (after his retirement) on October 28, 2006. Nelson went on to fight Mike Tyson and some other good heavyweights, as well as appearing as the June 1988 centerfold in Playgirl magazine!

"*Conroy Nelson guessed he's only about four pounds heavier than the night he fought Mike Tyson two decades ago. The cheerful 6-foot-6 Jamaican, however, isn't sure because he certainly doesn't own a scale and he can't afford to see a doctor. 'I need help, but nobody is around when the fun stops,' Nelson said. 'I can't even purchase a prescription. It's money I don't have. Right now I'm just in Jamaica all alone, trying to make a go of it.' (Mike) Tyson's 13th professional* *foe lives alone in a hut he constructed himself in St. Mary, near the chic resort town of Ocho Rios. The frame is made of bamboo, the roof of zinc. The floor is dirt. No plumbing. No electricity. No windowpanes. Nelson has no income aside from the tomatoes, corn, bananas, mangoes and sugar cane he grows and sells to neighbors and friends. He said he eats only 'what I catch and what I dig.' He doesn't own a car. He barely can afford the occasional $10 U.S. fee for minutes on his cell phone. He retired in 1998 with a record of 21-24-2 and 13 knockouts. He fought Trevor Berbick, Razor Ruddock, Alex Stewart, Bert Cooper, Herbie Hide and Riddick Bowe, losing to them all. Nelson also made some scratch playing bit roles in a few movies."* [20]

While Howard Darwin maintained that Conroy Nelson always *"lied like a rug"*, there was generally a wee bit of truth in most of what Conroy said. Take the acting reference made in the above ESPN lookback interview for example. According to IMDb (they bill themselves as 'the world's largest collection of movie, TV and celebrity information'), there was a Conroy Nelson who briefly appeared in ONE 1999 episode of "Honey, I Shrunk the Kids: The TV Show" (1997-2000) as "Third Beefy Man"! The short-lived TV series was filmed in Calgary.

A couple of Howard Darwin's better known friends however who would have met Nelson through Howard did have something that could be described as acting experience though. Boxer George Chuvalo and news anchor Mike Anscombe both spent more meaningful time in front of the movie lens than Conroy Nelson ever did. To date Chuvalo has over twenty movie credits and Anscombe at least six.

In April of 1986 Howard Darwin received and rejected an offer from the Edmonton Oilers to purchase the London Gardens arena and the London Knights hockey team. The Oilers had wanted to move their AHL team, the Nova Scotia Oilers to London. In 1987, Howard gave up fighting City of London officials who were refusing to extend city bus service an extra three kilometers to the Gardens, and sold his aging arena and his hockey team that was struggling with attendance problems at the time. Howard Darwin and Claude Bennett finally sold the London Knights and the London Gardens to Jack Robillard, Bob Wilson and Al Martin of Paris, Ontario for $2.3 million in 1987. A condition of Howard's on the sale was that the new owners keep the team in London.

In May of 1987 Howard Darwin suffered a physically debilitating stroke that left him with one weakened side and a pronounced limp that permanently limited his walking endurance. Howard stubbornly refused to use a cane afterwards.

With the arrival of the 90s, Howard Darwin corrected an earlier mistake with the official jersey retirement of Howard's favourite - and the Ottawa 67's most famous and talented hockey graduate: Denis Potvin from Overbrook. By January of 1990, Potvin had already won rookie of the year plus three Norris trophies as the NHL's top defenceman, while leading his New York Islanders to four straight Stanley Cups in the early 80s. Asked why it had taken him so long to retire Potvin's jersey, Howard simply said: *"I goofed, it's as simple as that. There were times I thought, geez, I have to retire his number, I'll get on it now, then, you know how it is, something else comes up and you put it off."* [21]

So, on Friday, January 26, 1990, Howard Darwin brought Denis Potvin and his family back to Ottawa where Potvin donned his familiar number seven Ottawa 67's barber pole jersey for a civic reception in the assembly hall at the Civic Centre, followed by the official ceremony at centre ice before the 67's game that night to officially retire his junior hockey number forever in Ottawa. For his part the articulate Potvin didn't seem too concerned about the late timing of his junior jersey retirement, because as the festivities wrapped up that evening, he took off the last Ottawa 67's number "7" jersey ever made, and handed it to his friend Howard Darwin saying, *"Thank you for everything Howard"*. That iconic jersey now belongs to Howard Darwin's grandson, Brad Darwin. (pg. 106)

Despite ample access to many famous athletes in particular, Howard Darwin didn't see past the real people in any of them and he rarely collected autographs or memorabilia. A chance hotel encounter and drink invitation from the Rolling Stones was met with *"no thanks"* from Howard (he claimed he didn't know who they were). Upon meeting Walter Gretzky in Sault Ste. Marie in 1977, he 'helpfully' told the father of the 'can't miss' pro prospect that he thought his son might be too small to play in the NHL!

The only personally signed picture that found its way onto a wall in Howard's office was a November 1975 Muhammad Ali. There were things of course that Howard put aside that he believed might be useful to his grandchildren someday, like the unique London Knights hockey stick coat racks now in the rooms of Jackie and Allie, and in particular the London Gardens 'house piano' that Brad, Jackie and Allie all learned to play on. Howard was especially proud of the fact that the old upright on wheels had been played at the London Gardens by countless circus troops and was routinely used as the warm up instrument backstage by the likes of Burton Cummings, Randy Bachman, Harry Belafonte, Nat King Cole, Isaac Hayes and even Liberace!

One of Howard's often repeated concert stories was of the night he watched Johnny Cash propose onstage to June Carter in the winter of 1968 at his London Gardens. Many years later Howard watched the Johnny Cash biographical movie "Walk the Line" to see if the movie director got it right, but was disappointed when the scene's subtitle simply read: "London, Canada".

Howard Darwin also had his share of speeding tickets, and on one trip through the United States he was caught for both speeding and for using his prized new dashboard radar detector. The State Trooper that pulled him over confiscated Howard's radar detector but offered to return it to him if he were to drop by to the police station on the return trip home. Howard did make the detour and returned to the station on his way back as suggested, only to be handed his unrecognizable radar detector in innumerable small pieces in a paper bag. It had been destroyed as required by state law, although the State Trooper forgot to mention that fact beforehand!

Howard Darwin's final closed circuit boxing event was the much hyped (and once delayed due to a Cooney injury), Larry Holmes and Gerry Cooney heavyweight championship fight on Friday, June 11, 1982 live from Las Vegas. Howard purchased the closed circuit rights for all of Canada for $600,000 from Don King for this last big production that became a fight promotion coup of sorts - when Howard beat out Toronto's Irving Ungerman for the Canadian closed circuit rights. Irving was incensed: *"I've never lost (the Canadian closed-circuit rights) before, but I lost this one because it was priced too high,"* Ungerman told The Globe and Mail's Robert MacLeod. Darwin couldn't resist a little gloating at Canada's reigning boxing impresario's expense: *"Its all sour grapes because he (Ungerman) didn't get the rights. You know what Irv's like. He thinks its his God-given right to promote every fight in Canada. What Irv needs is a little competition."*[22]

The marquee Holmes vs. Cooney fight also gave Howard an opportunity to return a few favours to his friends with regional 'promoters' like lawyer Larry Kelly (for Sudbury), broker Whit Tucker (Kingston), Western Hockey League's Ed Chynoweth (Calgary) and broadcaster Mike Anscombe (Sarnia). Even Howard's youngest son got in on the act: *"First-time promoter Jeff Darwin of Ottawa put on an impressive show at the Cornwall Civic Complex last night. The show, headlined by Larry Holmes' victory over Gerry Cooney, went off without a hitch. There were 872 people in attendance. According to 19-year-old Darwin, Cornwall viewers paid the lowest ticket prices ($15 and $20) in Canada."*[23]

In the summer of 1998, sixty-seven-year-old Howard Darwin and his long-time partner Earl Montagano sold the Ottawa 67's to Newfoundland carpet cleaning entrepreneur Jeff Hunt for $1.7 million. At the time it was the highest amount ever paid for a major junior hockey franchise in Canada. Howard had done well he thought with the $5,000 that Bill Touhey had lent him thirty-one years earlier!

(19) Scanlan, Wayne: The Ottawa Citizen; pg. F1, Jun 15, 1993
(20) Graham, Tim: 'Nelson Living in a Hut in
Jamaica'; Sports.ESPN.go.com, Jun 11, 2005
(21) McRae, Earl: The Ottawa Citizen; pg. xx, Jan 24, 1990
(22) MacLeod, Robert: The Globe and Mail; pg. S4, Jun 10, 1982
(23) Dryden, Steve: Standard-Freeholder; pg. 2, Jun 12, 1982

JEFF DARWIN

Conroy Nelson with Gerry Cooney, Greg Gayle, Howard Darwin boxing cartoon, Muhammed Ali

In 1962: Howard Darwin with his boxing Idol; "The Brown Bomber" (Joe Louis 1914-1981)

JEFF DARWIN

The 'chicken livers place', Denis Potvin, Howard Darwin Jewellers

X - CORNERMEN HAVE THEIR SAY

In the great tradition of squared circle sports (boxing and wrestling), and the many colourful characters of the Ring, Howard Darwin rarely pulled his punches when he had something to say to you because he hadn't "just fallen off the turnip truck".

If you were cheap, Howard would say *"you throw around nickels like manhole covers"*, and if you complained about your personal situation with children or relationships, he would often quip *"that's the screwing you get for the screwing you got"*. About his own children and the company he hoped they would *not* keep, Howard would warn *"if you play in the dirt you'll get dirty"*. Regarding finicky children at mealtime: *"it's a long time 'till breakfast"*, or *"it all goes down the same hole"* and *"you'll eat dirt before you die you know."*

If Howard Darwin really trusted you, like he trusted Joe Fagan, Bill Long, Earl Montagano, Claude Bennett or Brian Kilrea, you were *"as honest as the day is long"*. If Howard didn't trust you, he *"wouldn't want to be stuck in the desert with you holding the water bottle"*. When a promotion didn't sell well, Howard was known to borrow a saying from his fellow promoter and Western Canada counterpart, Nick Zubray: *"that town wouldn't spend a nickel to watch Christ wrestle a grizzly bear"* - which is probably also where Howard derived his many remarks from 'back in the day', which was really when *"Christ was a cowboy"*.

In business there were many people who believed in and trusted Howard Darwin with his crazy ideas and some of their own money - like Bill Touhey for example. In boxing terms these are your most important supporters and are known as your 'Seconds', and for prize fighters, the loneliest time starts with the Timekeeper shouting "SECONDS OUT!", followed by the sound of the bell to start the round. At that moment you are entirely alone with your opponent and there is simply nowhere to hide, nowhere to run, no one to pass off to. Like the prize fighter that he wanted to be, Howard Darwin welcomed that measure of personal accountability and complete control over the outcome of his many battles in life.

To encourage and guide a fighter after the sound of the bell for the next three minutes in a round of boxing from outside the ring, you have your Cornermen (or Seconds). These are the ones who have pushed, helped, cajoled and fully supported you up to this point. In Howard Darwin's amazing story, there were many in his corner. Here then, is what some of the Cornermen in Howard Darwin's remarkable life have had to say about this fighter over the years:

Larry Kelly (friend, lawyer and early neighbour) *"On a very personal level - as a youngster I wore a brace for almost three years. It was a huge thing from above my waist to just above my foot. When it was finally time to get this thing off me, word got around the neighbourhood and the first person at my door with a hockey stick was Howard Darwin."*

Bill Long (Ottawa 67's and London Knights coach) *"He's just a super guy to work for."*

Peter Laframboise (original Ottawa 67's player) *"We may not have won a lot of games, but I remember when Howard gave us nice red jackets with the 67's crest on them. If nothing else, we were the best dressed team in the league."*

Murray Wilson (original Ottawa 67's player) *"He always kept his word over anything and everything."*

Mike Moran (young neighbour) *"The Darwin house was always the hub of activity and I seemed to be near the epicenter most of the time. Mr. Darwin introduced my dad and I to Prime Minister Diefenbaker at a closed circuit boxing event. He brought me into the dressing room of the 67's and let me lace up future NHL players, I sat court side when the Harlem*

Globetrotters came to town and got pulled on court to be part of the show. As kids we saw a grizzly bear in their lane way that was a feature wrestling event at Landsdowne Park. All events that I will cherish forever. The fondest memories I have, are of my drop in hello's that would last for hours and how easy conversation and stories would flow."

Gord McCormick (hockey player) *"I have many fond memories of Howard and how well he treated us as players for the 67's in the early years."*

Frank Tunney (Toronto fight promoter) *"Howard was always high-class. His word was good, and that tells it all. Everybody from this area knew him and wanted to go there because they would be treated well."*

Dave Branch (OHL Commissioner) *"Howard had a vision in pretty well everything he did in life when you look at the success he enjoyed both in private business and the sports industry. And certainly with the OHL, his vision was very much a part of our growth and evolution."*

Blake Dunlop (hockey player) *"I had the great pleasure of meeting Howard as a 16 year old young man growing up in Ottawa, given the chance to play for the 67's for 4 years. He provided so much for so many as a person and civic leader!"*

Brian Kilrea (Ottawa 67's coach) *"His word was his bond. That was it. Everything didn't always work out right, but he was able to do so many things because everyone knew him and trusted him. Players left this club with total respect for the organization and it comes from strong leadership. That's what it's all about."*

Earl Montagano (business partner) *"Howard's very easy to work with and he respects other people's points of view. Many people have said that for two guys to get along for so long and so well is remarkable. We get along better than brothers often do."* (pg. 114)

Claude Bennett (friend, business partner) *"Howard came from very humble beginnings and achieved incredible success in all aspects of his life. And despite the success that he had, Howard never changed – he just never changed."* (pg. 114)

Gordon Henderson (friend, business partner) *"I would describe Howard as a man with foresight and vision. He's always been at the forefront of new things."*

Gord Hamilton (Ottawa-Nepean Canadians Sports Club) *"About the best characteristic I can think of in Howard is that he's never forgotten* about what's good for the community. If people say 'yeh, but he's made money from his sporting ventures' then they have no idea of who Howard Darwin really is." (pg. 114)

Bobby Smith (hockey player) *"And most of all I believe in people like Howard Darwin and Earl Montagano and Brian Kilrea."*

Joey Sandulo (Beaver Boxing Club) *"I don't have the words to articulate everything Howard has done for people in this community. Howard has done an awful lot for an awful lot of people, not only in sports, but in other things…like just plain life. Howard and I have been together in boxing since the 50s and now I can't seem to put into perspective what it all means. I just can't find the words to properly express all he has helped. You know, Howard was one of a kind. He really was."*

Jim Durrell (friend, Mayor of Ottawa) *"Howard wasn't born with a silver spoon in his mouth. He's earned everything through hard work (and) when Howard gets committed to something, he's tenacious. He's like a dog with a bone; he won't let go."* (pg. 114)

Jim Watson (Mayor of Ottawa) *"Howard Darwin made significant contributions to our community in both business and sport. I'm hopeful that community members and council share the desire to recognize Mr. Darwin for all he has done."*

Claude Brochu (President, Montreal Expos) *"Charles* (Bronfman, Expos owner) *did some checking* (because) *he didn't know Howard, and everybody he talked to said that he was an outstanding citizen and businessman. A man of his word. Ottawa needed our support and we jumped on it."*

Wayne McIntyre (professor, sports fan) *"He made a big difference in many of our lives and made it possible for those of us that had challenges to live and enjoy life."*

Dave Gervais (son's friend) *"As a young kid I always wanted to be around Howard Darwin. I used to go to a lot of 67's games with his son and after the games Mr. Darwin would take me into the dressing room to meet the players and pick out a hockey stick. Afterwards we would go into one of the lounges and sit around and listen to Mr. Darwin and his friends tell stories. I remember feeling like a big shot. One story comes to mind: one year his son and I were in high school, our school, Sir John A MacDonald and rival Laurentian made it to the city finals in hockey at the Barbara Ann Scott Arena. After the first game the student rivalry was so intense between* the schools there was fighting in the stands so the city threatened to cancel the final. Mr. Darwin stepped up and paid for sufficient police so the final games could be played."

Steve Boston (Ottawa-Nepean Canadians Sports Club) *"Working closely with Howard for the last years, he has taught so many life lessons that I am forever grateful."*

Don Campbell (friend) *"He got a kick out of how much bigger a world his grandchildren were experiencing than he would ever have experienced as a youngster or even a young man. His grandchildren were a huge part of his everyday world, and he couldn't get enough of them, or spend enough time with them."*

Stafford Rollocks (son's friend) *"I can remember one winter night Howard Darwin's son invited us over to his house; I was probably 15 years old. Mr. Darwin had people over, not just 'ordinary' people in my eyes but the movers and shakers of the time. I distinctly remember Mike Anscombe being there as well with other high profile people. Anscombe was the lead anchor on the number one rated sports recap show on Global TV and I recognized him immediately. As I was going to the basement to meet (Howard's son), Mr. Darwin called me over to introduce me to his guests and asked me to sit and stay awhile and join their conversation about hockey of course. I was over whelmed to be sitting there talking to Mike Anscombe about hockey. Howard Darwin has always treated me like I was his friend and not the friend of his son. That was the kind of person Mr. Darwin was; his son's friends were actually his friends as well. Mr. Darwin would also make sure that when the NHL came to Ottawa for pre-season games (Ottawa didn't have a team at that time) he would always make sure that we were invited to the games, with access to the players later for autographs. Last but not least, Mr. Darwin knew that I was a Montreal fan and that I loved Guy Lafleur, he gave me tickets to go to Montreal to see the Habs play against The Los Angeles Kings. That was my first time watching a live hockey game and to boot at the Montreal Forum. Those are memories that I will never forget. Mr. Darwin, regardless of who he was with or how busy he was always had time for the friends of family. He treated us like if we were his friend, for indeed we were."*

Joe Fagan (friend, business partner) *"If he liked you, he liked you, and if he didn't like you...well, I guess you were just out of luck. He took chances...*

chances that no one else would take. And usually he came out on top. We got along from Day One. We never had a disagreement. Never." (pg. 114)

Tony Bennett (son's friend) *"Howard Darwin had an undeniable and positive impact on the city, and there were some remarkable personal connections between our two families. My dad, Guy Bennett, was also a member of both the Ottawa Boys Club and later the Ottawa Nepean Canadians Sports Club, and knew Howard of course too. My dad was a 'Second' in Gale Kerwin's corner - a local fighter that Howard promoted a few times in Ottawa in the 50s - for some of Kerwin's fights, including one at Madison Square Garden. A 1964 Beatles closed circuit concert of Howard's at the old Auditorium in Ottawa was co-promoted with my mom's family business, the Galla Bakery. Years later I became a good friend of Howard's son Jeff. In 1992 I won the public contest to name the Ottawa Lynx and the prize was a trip to spring training in Florida. On that trip with me was my eldest son Steven, who became a bat boy for the Lynx in 1994 and later worked as a clubhouse manager and eventually head groundskeeper. Steven met his wife Julie when she also worked at Jetform Park and our youngest son Jordan eventually spent a summer there as a batboy too. I had the opportunity to see up close all the effort and time Howard spent on bringing the Lynx to Ottawa and operating a successful franchise. It never mattered what celebrity was in town, Howard would always go out of his way to introduce you. There was a great family feeling to be around Howard Darwin and the ballpark."*

There were also many business lessons to be gleaned from Howard's quips if you listened closely. On the subject of presentation or first impressions: *"You can charge $30 for a $15 watch if you put it in a $3 box"* (and complementary gift wrapping should always be included!), and *"When you meet people for the first time they'll always notice your hands and your feet. No one will buy what you're selling if you chew your finger nails or forget to shine your shoes."* On investing in land: *"They're not making any more of it"* and *"I wish I bought more."* On discounting your selling price: *"You'll never get $2 again for the ticket you just let go for $1."* On income taxes: *"I wish I were paying more taxes because that would mean I was making more for myself."* On employees and partners: *"Whose money is it?"* and *"Who will sleep better tonight?"*

While Howard Darwin himself usually had the last word - and you certainly always knew where you stood with him - there was one personal salutation that he insisted he leave you with: *"See you in church!"* But for the many that he couldn't say 'see you later' to in person, Howard had his standby song. The theme song from the 1977 movie "New York, New York" was recorded by Frank Sinatra in 1979 and this song, along with Sinatra's "My Way" were amongst Howard's favourites. From 1979 until 1998 at the Ottawa Civic Centre the organist was asked to play "New York, New York" as his final song to usher the hockey fans out to their cars. Same story for the Lynx games from 1993 until 2000: "New York, New York" on the organ or by the disk jockey; last song played…every game. No substitutions!

Earl Montagano, Claude Bennett, Gord Hamilton, Jim Durrell, Joe Fagan

XI – THE OTTAWA LYNX

Howard Darwin's final and most challenging personal accomplishment was the return of professional baseball to Ottawa after an absence of thirty-nine years, as well as the building of Ottawa's first major recreation venue since the opening of the Civic Centre in 1967, some twenty-six years earlier. Writer Terence Martin outlined the exhausting process in his spring 1993 story in the Ottawa Business Quarterly magazine entitled 'Anatomy of the Lynx – How the deal was done to bring Triple-A baseball to town':

"April 1988: The telephone rings at Howard Darwin Jewellers, a small but well-established store in Ottawa's west end, where self-made businessman, sports promoter and entrepreneur Howard Darwin keeps his office. It's Jim Durrell calling. "Howard," says Durrell, then-mayor of the city that is landlord to Darwin's Ottawa 67's junior hockey club, "Why don't you come down to my office for a chat?" With no clue as to what it's all about, Darwin drives out to City Hall. The lease. It must be the 67's lease. But –surprise – the topic is baseball, not hockey. A bemused Darwin listens as Durrell makes his pitch. Ottawa needs a Triple-A baseball franchise, with Darwin as owner.

After struggling with low attendance during the 1970s, minor league ball has never been more popular, and with major league expansion on the horizon, cities across North America are lining up for a shot at a franchise. For Ottawa, it's an opportunity that may not come again. Durrell is persuasive. A stadium will need to be built. The stadium will be a Good Thing for the community. Little League teams from the region will be able to play ball here, and a modern new facility would be available for different team sports and other forms of entertainment. Darwin questions the cost of acquiring a Triple-A ball franchise. The figure of $1.2 million is discussed. Darwin promises to think about it.

October 1988: The Mayor's office announces that a delegation from the city will travel to the baseball winter meetings in Atlanta to make a presentation to Triple-A ball club owners and league officials. So far Darwin's name hasn't publicly come up.

December 1988: Darwin announces his intention to purchase a minor league franchise that would eventually be based in Ottawa. It would be up to the city to see that a stadium is financed and built. Approval from the Triple-A Alliance to move the team to Ottawa would, presumably, be forthcoming, once these first two hurdles had been cleared. But which would come first, the franchise or the ballpark? There's also another factor to consider: it seems the price of a Triple-A franchise is on the order of $3 to $5 million, a far cry from the $1.2 million figure tossed out a year ago. Howard Darwin is undeterred. His pitching arm is just getting warmed up.

January 1989: Back from a fact finding mission to the U.S., city culture and recreation commissioner Don Gamble says that Ottawa needs to spend $36,000 to study two possible sites for a Triple-A ballpark. Also needed is a $10,000 study to sample Ottawans' feelings about Triple-A ball. At this stage, several aldermen are already balking at all this baseball talk. But the studies are approved.

November 1989: It is one year since the city officially announced its interest in minor league ball, and it's been a busy one for Darwin. He's been to the U.S. several times to look into buying a team, and travel costs are mounting. City council meets to consider proposals for Triple-A stadium sites at NCC-owned LeBreton Flats, the city's Bayview Road maintenance yard and a Riverside Park location. The proposal for the favored Bayview site includes a projected $15.9 million price tag, with a $4 million share from the city, an additional $4 million from the Ontario Government and $7.9 million through corporate sponsorships. But council is split on the Bayview site, with opponents citing hidden costs and local residents' concerns about noise, traffic and increased property taxes.

December 20, 1989: Council rudely awakens Darwin from his field of dreams with a 9 – 7 vote to reject the Bayview yards proposal. Mayor Durrell says petty politics doomed the site, and Darwin says "That's it. It's done and I'm done." There's no joy for Triple-A supporters in Ottawa.

January 1990: While area ball fans continue to vent their frustrations over the failure of council to agree on a stadium location, Alderman Darrell Kent, a Triple-A supporter, reveals that regional councilors have been involved in secret discussions on the possible involvement of the regional government in Triple-A ball.

March 1990: Durrell is on his way home from a meeting in the east-end when his driver, Lenny "the Snake" Cregan, turns onto the Vanier Parkway, near the Queensway and Coventry Road. All of a sudden Durrell has Cregan stop the car. "Snake" he says, looking out the window at the 19-acre patch of land across from RCMP Headquarters, "There's the perfect place for a baseball stadium." Back at City Hall, Durrell has staff find out who owns the property. Turns out its federally owned land, and the city enters into secret negotiations with Public Works Ministry to gain control of it.

June 18, 1990: With negotiations still underway, the City unveils plans for a new 10,000 seat Triple-A baseball stadium at a public meeting. The Coventry Road property has an appraised value of $11.5 million, while the projected cost of the stadium is $21.5 million. In return for the property, Ottawa would eventually agree to take over maintenance of 17 parks, roads and bridges from the NCC. The week after the plans are unveiled, Triple-A Alliance Commissioner Randy Mobley pops up in Ottawa, noting that 12 North American cities are now interested in the two planned expansion franchises. Darwin, Durrell and company are suddenly back in the swing of things.

July 4, 1990: Council votes to support the Coventry Road stadium proposal, even though estimates call for an expenditure of $10.7 million over 15 years to repair federal roadways such as Island Park Drive and the Queen Elizabeth Driveway. Residents in near-by Overbrook are split on the effect the stadium will have on the community. Just before leaving for the Triple-A All-Star game and more meetings in Las Vegas, Darwin has his commitment from the City firmly in hand.

August 23, 1990: Darwin's application for one of the two expansion franchises, with his U.S. $5,000 non-refundable cheque, makes it to Triple-A Alliance Headquarters in Columbus, Ohio ahead of all the others.

November 15, 1990: At the Triple-A expansion meetings in Chicago, Jim Durrell, Howard Darwin and Don Gamble make an hour-long presentation in their bid to acquire one of the two expansion franchises for Ottawa. The presentation is a success. Question marks remain, but over the last two years commissioner Mobley has become very familiar with Darwin and the Ottawa delegation and is comfortable with the progress to date. The big concern is the lack of a stadium so far, and the $13.2 million needed from the private sector to build it. The 1993 season is two and a half years away. It is expected that the two winners will be announced at the Triple-A All Star Game in July 1991.

February 15, 1991: Durrell, having assumed the presidency of the Ottawa Senators, resigns from city politics after mounting concerns about conflict of interest. Darwin has lost his "biggest booster on council." Meanwhile, Ottawa Triple-A Baseball Inc. has season ticket pledge coupons put in local newspapers, and fans can now put down $25 on a seat for the 1993 season.

August 15, 1991: An expected $4 million provincial grant for the construction of the stadium turns out to be half that amount, prompting an emergency council meeting where city politicians vote to give Triple-A Alliance commissioner Mobley written assurance that the stadium will be built, if Ottawa's application for an expansion franchise is approved. But city staff are scrambling to find areas to cut several million dollars from the cost of construction. Darwin, meanwhile, is cheered by the news of the City's letter to Mobley.

September 28, 1991: Success! Darwin's dream of bringing a Triple-A baseball franchise to his hometown is realized with the approval of the Triple-A Alliance to award one of the two expansion franchises to Ottawa. Darwin, vindicated, says: "I said all along that if somebody could convince me Triple-A baseball was bad for Ottawa, I'd call it quits. Nobody did." The agreement is already in place for the Montreal Expos to move their Triple-A farm team to Ottawa for the 1993 season. With the price for a franchise now at U.S. $5 million, Darwin must now make a down payment of $1.5 million, more than the (entire) price originally discussed during that long-ago conversation with Durrell.

March 18, 1992: The Ottawa Sun announces the winner (Tony Bennett) in a contest to name Ottawa's Triple-A ball club. The name of Ottawa's team is the Ottawa Lynx.

April 1, 1992: The Lynx get a general manager, Tom Maloney, a former manager of the Denver Zephyrs Triple-A ball club and more recently manager of the Birmingham Bandits basketball club.

June 19, 1992: Construction begins on the future home of the Lynx. Architects are Kohler Dickey Edmundson Matthews, whose Tremblay Road offices are within sight of the Coventry Road location. Bad weather and strikes play havoc with the construction schedule in one of the rainiest summers on record. Holders of the 5,000 ticket pledges select their seats.

December 14, 1992: Michael Quade is introduced as the Lynx' first field manager. Quade has been with the Expos since 1987. Quade (pronounced Kway-dee) most recently managed the Harrisburg, Pennsylvania AA ball club.

February 4, 1993: Lynx GM Maloney confirms that construction on Ottawa's Triple-A ball park is right on schedule, and that the stadium will be ready, except for some cosmetic touches, by April 1.

April 8, 1993: Season opener as the Ottawa Lynx visit the Charlotte, North Carolina Knights. The two Triple-A expansion franchise teams are both winners.

April 21, 1993: Charlotte visits Ottawa for the Lynx' home opener. Everyone seems ready for The Show."[24]

The above timeline suggests that Howard Darwin's journey to build a new ballpark and return professional baseball to Ottawa after a very long absence was relatively easy – it certainly was *not* so. Howard maintained that it was the most difficult and significant of all of his business accomplishments, particularly in satisfying the many objections and conditions of some of the City of Ottawa Councillors who were opposed at the time. Nine different times Howard Darwin faced the full City Council and only three times were the baseball-related motions passed as presented. At least three different sites were proposed by city staff for their new ballpark and then were subsequently rejected by full Council including Lebreton Flats, Bayview Yards and Riverside Park. The one constant in the incessant wavering of support from city hall over the five years leading up to Triple-A baseball however was Don Gamble, Commissioner of Recreation and Culture. Howard and Don would become good friends.

"*Facing adversity is nothing new for Darwin. He fought with city hall about the construction of the Landsdowne Park complex while trying to bring the 67's to Ottawa, as well as during his battle to establish the capital's first cable company, Ottawa Cablevision. And he can recount the struggles associated with his first business, a watch repair shop on Nicholas Street, and his experiences as a kid selling newspapers on Lisgar Street during the Second World War."* [25] New personal Ten Counts for Howard had to be beaten each time, and it certainly aged the fighter from Nicholas Street well beyond his sixty-one years of age.

Howard Darwin certainly didn't need to start another major business at this stage of his life and certainly none of his family were encouraging him to embark on the return of professional baseball to Ottawa. A quote of Howard's from a 1988 newspaper column summarized his motivations at the time: *"I love this town. I think a ball club would be good for the town. It'll bring money in, create business and jobs, make the place livelier. We have to get a franchise to get a stadium, and I think a stadium would be good for Ottawa. I mean a nice one, 10,000 seats, lots of parking, right up to date, state of the art. I don't mean only for baseball, but for all kinds of things. And it won't mean so much to us, for our generation, but for my kids, and their kids. It'll be good for Ottawa, and minor league baseball is doing well all over the continent."* [26]

After closing the front doors of Howard Darwin Jewellers on March 28, 1992 after thirty-seven years in the same west end location, Howard and his *"right and left hand"* for almost as long, Joe Fagan, moved upstairs at 1308 Wellington Street once more to start a professional baseball team from scratch this time. Howard later admitted privately that *"I despised the jewellry business."* One of the first moves made by the fledgling baseball owner and the experienced ticket manager was acting on the recommendations of some of his fellow International League owners, and hiring the 1991 minor league executive of the year from the Triple-A Denver Zephyrs of the Pacific Coast League. The hiring of Tom Maloney as the team's first General Manager was a significant and early mistake for Howard right out of the gate.

Joining Joe Fagan (box office) and rounding out a trusted inner circle of familiar faces at Ottawa Stadium (as it was initially called; later Jetform Park and finally Lynx Stadium), were former Ottawa 67's trainer John Bryck (as Lynx clubhouse manager), Jack Darwin (stadium operations), Nancy Darwin (Lenny's Boutique) and Rupert Darwin (program sales).

The Ottawa Lynx first General Manager Tom Maloney certainly didn't lack confidence, and as Howard Darwin quickly found out, he was a pro at spending other people's money too. Shortly after Maloney's arrival in Ottawa, Howard started getting phone calls from American debt collectors and process servers. The beginning of the end for Tom Maloney occurred just weeks after he moved into one of the Lynx temporary offices - upstairs from Howard's old jewellry store at 1308 Wellington Street - when Howard received a call from Canada Customs and Immigration.

The Immigration folks were holding one "Dave Maloney", brother of Tom Maloney at the Ogdensburg, NY border crossing, and they were asking Howard to confirm the offer of employment letter that Howard had apparently signed, and that Dave Maloney had just presented to Immigration authorities to get into Canada pulling a trailer-load of personal possessions. Howard knew nothing about Dave Maloney or the employment offer, and had never signed the letter, and now he was on the spot. With Immigration on hold, and Howard unable to find his new GM Tom Maloney, who had left the office earlier telling Lynx staff that he had to drive to Prescott to pick up some 'equipment' he had ordered, Howard very reluctantly said "yes", please let him through. The Ottawa Lynx first General Manager, Tom Maloney, and his brother and Assistant General Manager Dave Maloney, did make it through the Ottawa Lynx inaugural season, and were both fired as it ended by Howard Darwin on September 16, 1993; leaving a wake of unpaid rent, dry cleaning and other personal bills and promises behind them in Ottawa.

While it seemed forever in the making, the Ottawa Lynx inaugural game (an 8 – 6 Ottawa win) was played on the road against the Charlotte Knights on Thursday, April 8, 1993: *"The owner made his way to the dressing room where, true to form, he introduced **himself** to his players. There was no pomp and circumstance. No formal introductions. As more of the players came to Darwin and clenched hands with him, the more difficult it became to hold back his emotions…He paused, grabbed a handkerchief from a jacket pocket and wiped the collection of tears from around his eyes and cheeks."* [27] New Brunswicker Matt Stairs set aside his personal disappointment at being demoted from the Montreal Expos to the Ottawa Lynx earlier that day, and gave Howard Darwin his ball from the first hit ever made by an Ottawa Lynx player in franchise history.

Opening day in Ottawa was equally emotional for Howard Darwin. On April 17, 1993, a scrappy, first year roster of players like Curtis Pride, Rondell White, Todd Haney, Mark Grudzielanek, Shane Andrews, Derek Lee, Derek Aucoin, Kirk Rueter and fan favourite, F. P. Santangelo (Santangelo went on to have his jersey #24 retired by the Lynx, and to have a seven year major league career with the Expos, Giants, Dodgers and Athletics).

In their inaugural 1993 season, the Ottawa Lynx sold out every single one of their seventy-two home games to set an International League of Professional Baseball Clubs attendance record of 693,043 paid admissions in one season. This attendance record appears to still be standing. The following season was thirty-six Lynx home game sell-outs (596,858 paid attendance), and the 1995 league championship season was just eleven sell-outs for 511,865 total paid for the season. Ottawa Lynx team performance on the field declined significantly after the 1995 championship season and Howard was exhausted.

In Howard Darwin's final season owning the Ottawa Lynx just 195,979 Ottawa fans paid to see the team play professional baseball in the nation's capital. The Lynx were bleeding red ink by season four, the City of Ottawa as their landlord were becoming increasingly difficult to deal with. Howard Darwin was growing weary promoting professional baseball in Ottawa.

The family atmosphere around Lynx Stadium for the Darwins was great in the early 90s with Howard's children and grandchildren having full run of the complex. The work days were still very long for Howard however, and at sixty-five years of age following the 1995 season – and each net dollar earned going directly to the City of Ottawa to satisfy his financial commitments to them – Howard was beginning to contemplate a well-earned retirement. On April 24, 1995, Howard Darwin was saddened by the death of his younger friend and most ardent City of Ottawa staff supporter, Don Gamble, from cancer.

On the 1995 evening that the Ottawa Lynx with manager Pete Mackanin won their only International League Championship just three years into their history, F. P. Santangelo and Canadian Joe Siddall had been late season call ups to Montreal. Both jumped into a car un-showered after a game in Montreal and rushed down Highway #417 back to Ottawa to celebrate with their Lynx teammates and the fans of Ottawa. The professional baseball championship was a major sports highlight for the city.

The City of Ottawa continued to sell-off parts of the stadium lands that it acquired from the federal government for its Coventry Road development in the second half of the 90s, which compounded Howard's baseball attendance struggles through reduced on-site parking. Canadian interest in baseball in general was also waning, particularly for the Lynx parent Montreal Expos, and the Ottawa Lynx were playing terribly.

So in June of 2000 Howard Darwin sold his expansion Triple-A baseball franchise to American Ray Pecor for $5.5 million USD (just a 9% total capital gain over seven years owning the franchise), and paid off the remaining balance on his commitment to the City of Ottawa to construct their new $16.9 million dollar ballpark built in 1992-1993.

Over the course of seven years, Howard Darwin directed a total of $17,554,445 to flow back to the taxpayers of the City of Ottawa from Ottawa Lynx revenues. He lost a significant amount of personal money developing Coventry Road for the city - so with his financial obligations to local taxpayers now paid in full - Howard felt compelled to carry a copy of the City's full and final release with him signed by year 2000 Mayor Jim Watson and City Clerk Pierre Pagé. The document was necessary to counter the few politicians and columnists who had forgotten that this stretch of Coventry Road had only a derelict former bottling plant and a snow dump before Howard Darwin and Jim Durrell brought professional baseball back to Ottawa.

(24) Martin, Terence: 'Anatomy of the Lynx' Ottawa Business Quarterly; pg. 13 – 19, Spring 1993
(25) Henderson, Mark: 'His Biggest Catch Yet' Ottawa Business Magazine; pg. 26, Jan / Feb 1992
(26) MacCabe, Eddie: The Ottawa Citizen; pg. B2, Dec 11, 1988
(27) Campbell, Barre: The Ottawa Sun; pg. 14, Apr 11, 1993

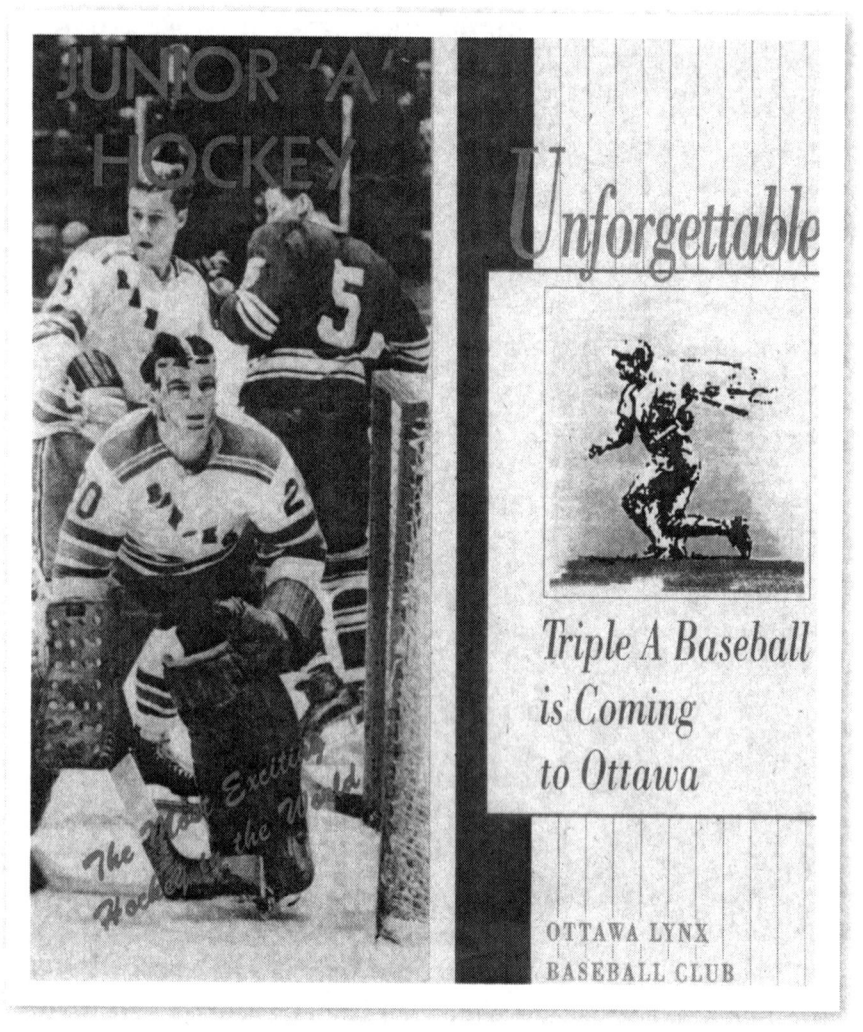

*Initial brochures used to bring Major Junior A Hockey
(1967) and Professional Baseball (1993) to Ottawa*

Inaugural front office staff for the Ottawa Lynx (1993)

JEFF DARWIN

*Howard Darwin and his 1995 International
League Champion Ottawa Lynx*

XII – RETIREMENT

With Howard Darwin's sale of the Ottawa 67's in 1998 followed by his sale of the Ottawa Lynx in 2000, it was truly time for the sixty-nine-year-old to slow down and enjoy the fruits of his labour. Although his retirement plans had always been to travel, poor mobility from a heart attack, stroke and a broken hip limited Howard's endurance for travel.

But he did get to the South Pacific to see for himself the beauty that his older brother Percy had told him about from the deck of his corvette during the war.

Retirement gave Howard's friends a chance to learn more of what his immediate family already knew: Howard Darwin loved Labatt's 50th Anniversary Ale, and would avoid establishments that didn't serve this less popular of the Labatt brands. Howard maintained that being less popular than other brands had the advantage of ensuring that "50" had been in the fridge longer and would therefore be colder! Howard felt that any meal served after 11AM should be accompanied by an ice cold bear (or three) from a can (again, supposedly colder), and never with water or wine. Late in life Howard did relent just a little when he discovered 'Nouveau Beaujolais' red wine in single-serving bottles which he would keep in the fridge next to his Labatt's 50 - and drink equally cold with his dinner!

Howard Darwin loved Chinese food from Sampan, Yinny's, Golden Palace or the Won Ton House – but never from anywhere else. Howard loved Malbec oysters, and each month that they were in season he would have Lapointe's hold out a full wooden crate of them which he would lug home, drop on the kitchen floor and devour raw on the half shell drenched in Tabasco sauce in one sitting! Only later in life did Howard's doctor, Rudy Gittens, have the nerve to tell him that the frequent bouts of excruciating gout in his feet and ankles were caused by his oysters!

Live dinner shows or eating out were a real pleasure for Howard but he always refused to make reservations. His favourite tactic at busy restaurants was to confidently announce the current time at the front counter and *"Reservation for Darwin!"*, with a pause and a slightly louder follow up of *"You haven't lost my reservation have you?"* To the great embarrassment of his dinner companions it generally worked, but when it didn't a folded banknote palmed to the Maître 'D, Pit Boss or Manager usually did the trick!

Howard Darwin disliked wearing ties but he loved to dress well. He hated golf and he loved his big cars. It was for safety he would say, and *"I'd drive a tank if they sold them"*. Howard preferred Chrysler Imperials or Lebarons, and later on Cadillacs. In retirement he took up Mercedes sedans on the recommendation of his grandson Ben, who sold him on the German engineering. Ben was always Howard's go-to grandchild for all things automotive or yard maintenance related. Howard loved to listen to Frank Sinatra tapes on the road for favourites like "New York, New York" and "My Way" (written by Ottawa's Paul Anka).

On the subject of grandchildren, Howard Darwin had nine in total and he adored them all. He kept a close eye on each one of his grandchildren and could recount to his friends in remarkable detail what each one of them was up to at any given time. It was from his nine grandchildren that Howard Darwin earned the title that was most important to him: *Poppa*. An expert in gift wrapping from his days in retail, all the grandkids could spot a gift wrapped by their beloved Poppa!

Howard loved fishing, and for a time carried the incredible 'Popeil's Pocket Fisherman' in the glove box of his car - just in case he needed to get out to stretch his legs near a pond or stream. As a youth Howard plied the Rideau, Ottawa and Gatineau Rivers, as well as the lakes of Eastern Ontario and Western Quebec. As an adult Howard fished for salmon in Newfoundland and pickerel in Northern Ontario where his regular fishing party first convened before they sailed further out on deep sea fishing trips from Florida.

Howard loved dealing in cash and always carried plenty. Whether he was purchasing something at an independent shop or at a major department store chain, he would always ask for the *"cash price"* of the item and maintained that it *"never hurts to ask"* (and he very often got his cash discount)!

Retirement also gave Howard Darwin an opportunity to slow down and reflect a little on his amazing life and to connect with great friends over a beer. For his golden years Howard had memberships in two private clubs in Ottawa, one being the prestigious Rideau Club and the other being the more street-level Ottawa Nepean Canadians Sports Club which continues to raise hundreds of thousands of dollars for amateur sport. Now the two clubs he belonged to could not have been more diverse. The Rideau Club overlooks Parliament Hill and is the domain of the movers-and-shakers, both in Ottawa and at the National Level. Go for dinner and you might be surprised to see what lawyer or businessman is sitting with what Cabinet Minister. The Rideau Club is home to successful professionals and Howard might well have been the only member with a grade nine education in the entire place. Its walls are lined with pieces of art and the woodwork is all oak.

Now the Sports Club, just a short drive east of Howard's long time residence, is located in an old strip mall, across the street from a garage and park and backs on to an affordable housing project. The members there are plumbers, sports fans, retirees, cops and firemen, tradesmen, even the odd sportswriter. Beer is cheap, food has to be ordered in from a nearby takeout place and the stories - and some say bullshit - flows endlessly. The walls are littered with old sports pictures hung on plaster and any woodwork is merely pine. Let it be said Howard was equally comfortable and maybe even favoured the Sports Club persona.

Howard once purchased a motorized golf cart there and drove it home just to see the reaction he would get from Connie and the grandkids!

In his later years, Howard became even more deeply involved with the Sports Club, lending his expertise and experience to lead the way towards setting the club on a better path to viability and continued prosperity. Howard was not loud but when he spoke it was a lot like E.F. Hutton: people listened. And Howard shared his opinions and his knowledge.

Just about every day around five the silver Mercedes would make it way down Iris Street and in through the door of the Ottawa Nepean Canadians Sports Club would walk Howard and he knew everyone and everyone knew him. He'd look for a bar stool and an ice cold Labatt "50" would hit the top of the bar before Howard had sat down. And the stories would start. Many of them were what could be described as the good old days in Ottawa, when it seemed it was nothing more than a small town where everyone knew everybody. Others would be funny stories about his interactions with other members, especially a few old retired cops. He loved to tell the one about the robbery at his jewelry store, a robbery investigated by now retired Detective Leonard Trombley, who worked directly under retired Inspector Doug "Pops" Thompson. The robbery, apparently, was never solved and no arrest was ever made. Often there would be Trombley and Thompson holding court at a large, round table with their co-horts when Howard walked through the door and deadpanned with an *"Any progress on catching the guy who robbed my store?"* Trombley, just as quick-witted, would fire back with: *"Well our surveillance team is following up on a couple of leads so it's really just a matter of time before we get him."* Now, considering the robbery took place thirty years ago, it would be instantaneous laughter all round.

Or it could be Ottawa Rough Rider legend Bobby Simpson being his usual loud self and Howard and he reminiscing about all the old drinking spots - even night spots - downtown and how much fun they had back in the day. It just never mattered what a person's background was. Howard was a people person and he loved to hear a story, be prompted to tell a story, or just answering a question on Ottawa trivia that no-one could get an answer for. Then about five minutes before 6 o'clock, Howard knowing the speed at which bartender Jack Gosselin moved, would ask for CJOH on the TV nearest to him. He never wanted to miss a second of the evening news with Max Keeping and Carol Anne Meehan. *"Any way you could turn it up?"* Howard would ask Jack. And for the next sixty minutes, everyone in the place would watch - and listen - to the six o'clock news, often with Howard's unsolicited 'colour commentary' on the events of the day. Howard was a newshound. His best job ever was selling newspapers as a boy, and into his final years he would read upwards of four or five newspapers a day. And not just the headlines. And if he was away for any length of time, the newspapers had to be saved for him to read when he got home.

But once J.J. Clarke delivered the weather forecast about 6:45, that was his cue to head for Malone Crescent and dinner with Connie. *"I better get there fast...before she burns it."* he would say, joking of course. And then *"Cash me out...and get one for yourself."* And off he would go... until tomorrow.

Howard felt comfortable at the Sports Club in control of the remote on his reserved stool surrounded by regulars like Bobby Bull and Steve Boston who pretended not to tire of hearing his old stories *again*. Invariably, the name Conroy Nelson would come up: "*Conroy Nelson was Howard Darwin's great heavyweight hope. Conroy was the guy Muhammad Ali wanted to look like. Conroy was a training-gym superman whose kryptonite was a particular sound – the sound of a bell to start the fight. 'It was a bigger dream than the baseball stadium,' says Joey Sandulo, who trained Nelson on Howard's behalf, 'to have the heavyweight champion of the world here in Ottawa. Conroy had everything going for him. All he needed was a heart transplant.' 'Ah, it wasn't that bad,' says Howard. 'Some people go to the track and play the horses. I had Conroy. It was an adventure'.*"[28]

In the company of a few friends Howard would comfortably hold court and tell stories all night long, but he was terrified of anything that approached public speaking. Howard could converse for an hour with an interesting street vendor he just met, or with any shoe shine boy he encountered on a walk as well. In New Orleans one time a young shoe shine boy talked Howard into an over-priced shine that he didn't need. Before he even got to *"Where you from?"*, the boy said

"Mister. I know where you got your shoes!" Howard couldn't resist taking the bait. *"Okay smart guy. Double or nothing on the shine if you can tell me where I got my shoes."* The shoe shine boy looked Howard up and down and pretended to concentrate, and then finally said: *"Mister. You got this shoe on my box and you got that shoe on the sidewalk."* The shine cost the Canadian tourist ten bucks but the experience was priceless to Howard Darwin – the former shoe shine boy from Nicholas Street.

In the late 1990s Howard Darwin finally stepped down from the Board of Trustees of the institution that he helped set up in 1967: the Ottawa Sports Hall of Fame. This constitutionally permitted Howard's own induction now into the Hall. Howard Darwin was one of seven inductees into the Ottawa Sports Hall of Fame in 1998. Other inductees that year were former NHL stars Doug Wilson (Chicago / San Jose) – a former Ottawa 67's player of Howard's – and Bill Touhey (Montreal / Boston), who had given Howard the original shop space to establish The Watch Clinic. Fittingly, Touhey had also worked with Howard Darwin in the beginning to establish the Ottawa Sports Hall of Fame itself, the Ottawa 67's, and the Ottawa Civic Centre in 1966 and 1967.

In only his second year of true retirement, 2002 brought Howard Darwin an unfortunate double-dose of personal loss with the death of his seventy-seven-year-old, older brother Percy, on May 3, 2002. On August 12, 2002 though, Howard was completely devastated by the unexpected death of his eldest daughter Kim, at the tender age of only forty-seven. The premature loss of his first child at the same age (forty-seven) that his own mother Mayme had died was almost too much for Howard to bear. Howard said repeatedly that: *"A parent should never have to bury a child."* With the two Ten Counts coming so close together, it was apparent to some that the fighter from Nicholas Street was weakening.

Howard's retirement also afforded him the opportunity to get back into many of the annual dinners and events that he was unable to faithfully attend when working. One of these events was the annual Village Reunion dinner held at the St. Anthony's Soccer Club on Preston Street. At one of these dinners however Howard tripped over a chair on the way to his table and broke his hip. Howard suffered through the dinner in severe pain and asked for assistance to his car at the end of the evening. His table-mates tried unsuccessfully to take him to the hospital, instead ending up at the Darwin family kitchen table for more late night beers. As the party broke up, Howard finally admitted that he could not move and somehow convinced his friends to carry him up to his bed – still completely immobilized in his kitchen chair!

When morning arrived the only one that the stubborn Howard would let Connie call was his 67s team doctor and friend, Mark Aubry. Fortunately for Howard, Dr. Aubry came right over to the house to see the clearly broken hip and called for an ambulance some twelve hours after the fall. Dr. Aubry called ahead to the civic to advise the top orthopedic surgeon in Ottawa that Howard was on his way in and required surgery. This was Howard's first introduction to orthopedic surgeon Dr. Don Chow who would also become a life-long friend and medical confidant.

On August 22, 2009 Howard and Connie were part-way through dinner at a west end pizzeria when Howard announced that he wasn't feeling well and that they were heading home now. Connie didn't argue once she noticed that Howard – quite uncharacteristically – had not finished his beer. Howard made it as far as the front door when he collapsed on Connie. He was rushed to the University of Ottawa Heart Institute where he was stabilized and heart surgery was performed within days. Sixty-one days later on October 22, 2009 - and having never left the hospital - Howard Darwin died from post-operative infection. Howard fought the fight of his life to celebrate his seventy-ninth and final birthday in the hospital, but could not beat **The Ten Count** in his final round.

Howard Darwin's funeral had to be televised locally by public demand. Five Ottawa Mayors, most local Newsmen and many local Sportsmen attended the service. The Darwin family and the Ottawa sporting community had lost a pioneer, historian and cherished patriarch.

(28) Scanlan, Wayne: *The Ottawa Citizen;* pg. F1, Jun 15, 1993

JEFF DARWIN

Howard Darwin loved fishing

THE TEN COUNT

*Store closing, grandchildren, with sons and Mathew
Hilton, a Village Reunion dinner*

Retirement, the Beaver Boxing Club

XIII – STANDING EIGHTS

Not every sports, entertainment or business venture that Howard Darwin touched turned to gold of course. In a boxing match your minor setbacks are sometimes marked by a referee's 'standing eight' or 'protection' count. In the early years Howard would have many of these.

Take Howard's rag picking business for example. As a boy selling newspapers during the war years, Howard got the idea to leverage the war rationing momentum and the scrap metal drives that were taking place to aid our efforts overseas. Howard tried to organize some friends to collect rags door to door after school, which Howard would then bundle and resell to the rag pickers. The new business failed because the kids were too unreliable, and Howard couldn't supervise them effectively while he and Rupert were manning their newsstands!

Shortly after meeting his future wife Connie Goudie, while working for Stephen – Harvey Jewellers in the spring of 1949, eighteen-year-old Howard struck upon the idea of selling dew worms by the dozen to local fisherman and families. One of Howard's earlier dates with Connie at that time wound down with a midnight session of worm picking on the grassy upper bank above the tracks on the west side of Nicholas Street in front of his house. Once the coffee cans were full, and Connie was thoroughly disgusted, the date night concluded with Howard proudly displaying his wash tub inventory of soil and dew worms behind his row house to his new girlfriend. This was surely a springboard to a successful business of his own! When Howard and Rupert subsequently spent a warm, early July weekend at their Aunt's hotel in Montreal, the wash tub dried out and the dew worm business died from the heat! Connie Goudie was unimpressed of course.

On the musical entertainment front, shortly after Howard Darwin Jewellers opened on Wellington Street in 1955, Howard also missed seeing anything special in a particularly annoying kid from the local high school who was coming into the jewellry store after school to pester Howard or Joe Fagan into purchasing an ad in the Fisher Park High School Yearbook. *"The little prick wouldn't take no for an answer,"* Howard would explain. *"Finally, I threw him out of the shop one day and told his uncle to tell the kid to stay away."* Paul Anka went on to do pretty well for himself in New York City after his encounter with Howard when Anka released his breakout song "Diana" the following year.

Promoting rock shows sometimes proved equally frustrating for Howard Darwin. In 1958 Howard had to refund a big crowd at the Auditorium when the house lights came up after the warm-up band's set, but never came down again because the headliner wouldn't come out of his dressing room. After several minutes with the rowdy house, Howard pushed his way past the handlers and band mates into Gerry Lee Lewis' dressing room to find the legendary piano player slumped in the corner and completely intoxicated. An enraged Darwin crossed the room and started kicking Gerry Lee Lewis until he was pulled off by his handlers. *"I was so mad I kicked him and told him he had a show to do and to get the hell up,"* Howard told us often. *"And I kicked him again and again when I was sure he wasn't going on stage! I had to refund all the money to the customers and I never had Gerry Lee back again."*

Only five months after the tremendous success of his 1958 St. Patrick's Day boxing event featuring Gale Kerwin and Davey Dupas, Howard Darwin partnered with an experienced Toronto promoter by the name of Loren Cassina for another major fight card at the Auditorium. On December 15, 1958, Darwin and Cassina 'lost their shirts' though when just 309 people showed up to see Dick Veronica knock out Ottawa's Johnny Massie in the main event, and J. D. Ellis earn a hard fought decision over Davey Dupas on the undercard.

Everything Howard had earned from his 5,000 person gate in March was lost by Christmas on his follow up promotion. Edward MacCabe, a sportswriter for the Ottawa Journal at the time, declared it 'the death of boxing in Ottawa'.

Howard Darwin's closed circuit arena broadcast events were often fraught with technical difficulties and the risks of 'no-show' fighters - or just poor entertainment value - like the September 1962 world heavyweight championship broadcast fiasco at the Auditorium when Floyd Patterson kissed the canvas early in the first round against Sonny Liston. There were many complaints and plenty of refund demands that evening.

In March of 1963 Howard Darwin promoted the closed circuit broadcast of the Cassius Clay vs. George Chuvalo fight live from Toronto, in the Coliseum building at Landsdowne Park. On that evening Howard probably wished that he was in Toronto himself with his childhood idol Joe Louis who was helping in the Canadian George Chuvalo's corner. The fight was great and Howard's 1,876 paid attendance made for a good gate that evening, however with everybody smoking in the Coliseum, the already blurry closed circuit picture gradually disappeared into a cigarette smoke haze!

With an Indianapolis 500 race event in the 60s, Howard Darwin speculated then how the car race must have got its name, when less than 500 people paid to watch it live on closed circuit television at the Coliseum. Howard was forced to rent the long distance telephone lines that would carry the Patterson-Liston heavyweight fight that he was promoting shortly after the Indianapolis 500 for a full thirty days from Bell Canada anyway.

One of Howard Darwin's biggest sporting regrets would come in March of 1966 when he came very close to staging a world heavyweight championship bout in Hull, Quebec. At the time Ottawa Citizen sports columnist (and future Ottawa 67's partner), Jack Kinsella, summed up the sentiments this way:

"It couldn't have been more than a nine-count after the bulletin announcing the bad news from Toronto when the telephone rang shrilly in Howard Darwin's jewelry emporium. 'Well, that's life,' muttered Darwin philosophically as he hung up the telephone. 'One minute I'm promoting a world

heavyweight championship, and the next I'm selling a $1.98 trophy. I don't think you could come any closer, even in fiction.' The final resolution of the off-again, on-again heavyweight fight between Cassius Clay and Ernie Terrell was a blow to the Ottawa boxing promoter who, up until the eleventh hour, had the fight *'locked up for the Hull Arena.' 'I talked by long distance telephone to Bob Arum, the lawyer for Main Bouts Inc., last night,'* revealed Darwin yesterday afternoon, *'and he was so certain the bout would be vetoed in Toronto that he told me to fill out an Ontario Commission contract in triplicate and have it ready. But I guess we underestimated the politicians.'* Arum and Darwin underestimated a lot of other people as well, including the vast ranks of the literary set which, almost without exception, went to the very end of the limb in suggesting that the fight was anathema and would never be held in any good, pious, and upstanding Canadian city. If Darwin was disappointed, it was an entirely understandable, if not human, reaction. Everybody has a secret ambition in life, and by his own admission, Darwin's longstanding aspiration was to promote a world heavyweight championship fight someday. *'Maybe I'll get another chance,'* he sighed, *'but I doubt if I'll ever come as close again, and lose out.'* If the plans had gone to fruition, Darwin would have received 30 per cent of the net at the Hull Arena – the arena was scaled to a figure of approximately $120,000 – out of which all the promotion expenses would have come. The fighters would have split the remainder, 50-20, in favor of Clay. There was some talk that Edmonton had the inside track if Toronto passed on the fight, but this has little substance. Hull was the site all the way, for reasons of television. *'Transmission from the west is a problem for closed circuit arrangements,'* explained Darwin, *'and Arum told me that next to Montreal or Toronto, our area would be best for the source of the signal.'* If the loss of the fight was a disappointment for Darwin, a close second blow was the feeling in some quarters that he was committing some sort of heinous crime in even considering the promotion. This sort of thinking, obviously, was the result of the wide refusal by the holier-than-thou set to entertain the fight anywhere within their precincts. *'You know,'* he admitted yesterday, *'for a few days I was almost bluffed into forgetting about it, especially when I was told I would be criticized. But then, quite by chance – and I realize this probably sounds ridiculous – I picked up a copy of the Bill of Rights. That settled it for me right there and then.'* Darwin's argument was that a man should do what he feels is right, no matter what the consequences, and that to act otherwise would be to equate oneself with the very people who oppose the action on various grounds, in this case mostly spurious. 'The way I looked at it,' he said, 'this would have been a good, if not logical fight, and the objections, really, were little more than political. In fact, what was worse, the political pressure was coming from the United States, and why should that affect what we do in Canada? If there had been anything unsavoury, or illegal, about the fight, I wouldn't have considered handling it for a minute'."* [29]

The Bill of Rights that Howard Darwin spoke of was Howard's treasured, personalized and signed copy of the bill his friend and fellow fight fan John Diefenbaker originally introduced into Canadian law as Prime Minister of Canada on March 29, 1960. In the world heavyweight championship fight that went to Toronto in 1966, Toronto's George Chuvalo was brought in as a late replacement for Ernie Terrell. Howard Darwin's most prized souvenir from this Standing Eight is a CN telegraph from Frank Sinatra's agent reserving 100 of Howard's $100 (top price) ringside seats at the Hull Arena!

In September of 1971, Howard Darwin got his last great chance at staging a major heavyweight boxing match in his hometown the following month, when he agreed to promote Muhammed Ali vs. Jerry Quarry in Ottawa: *"It's always been my life-long ambition in sports to promote a heavyweight championship fight here and while this isn't for the title it's the next best thing."* [30] Unfortunately, this fight never took place in Ottawa.

One of Howard Darwin's closed circuit boxing matches somehow became a 'front-page' international incident in February of 1967: *"A misunderstanding over Coliseum seats involving the Congolese ambassador last night is developing into an international incident. The ambassador, Pierre M'Bale, said today he will demand an apology from the external affairs department for the way he was treated at the closed-circuit Clay-Terrell fight in the Coliseum last night. The ruckus started when the 31 year old ambassador and his party were inadvertently placed in the wrong seats. The ambassador was asked to move, but he is objecting to the way the request was made. 'Mr. Congo, stand up and get out of here,' is the way he said he was asked to vacate the seats. 'I was highly upset. I told the usher, if you don't know my name you can call me sir or Mr. Ambassador. I'm not Mr. Congo any more than you're Mr. Canada.' When the security guard then moved behind him the ambassador and his party then left and called the police in the lobby. Police arrived and after some discussion the diplomatic party was given other seats. Ken McDonald, owner of Capital Guard Service, and his men saw Congo ambassador written on the tickets. Thinking this was the ambassador's name, he addressed him as Mr. Congo. Mr. McDonald said he later apologized to the diplomat but Mr. M'Bale refused to accept the apology."* [31]

Even the birth of Major Junior 'A' Hockey in Ottawa offered up some opportunities for Howard Darwin to miss. The March 12, 1967 letter from the coach of the Omaha Nights (Nebraska), was asking to be considered for the first Coach of the Ottawa 67's: *"The Memorial Cup is the only hockey trophy of any note that has escaped me. Otherwise I am very happy with my position now with the New York organization."* [32] Fred "The Fog" Shero went on to coach the Philadelphia Flyers to back to back Stanley Cups in 1974 and 1975. Shero is now in the Hockey Hall of Fame as a builder.

Possibly the most chilling of Howard Darwin's failed business ventures came from the boxing arena, where he had agreed to co-promote a live boxing event with a Montreal-based promoter whom Howard had not worked with before. The card was to be held in Montreal - and the promoter collected Howard's advertising and venue deposit money for that city in advance - and then was never heard from again. It was a lot of money for a struggling businessman to lose, however on the advice of Ottawa police Howard dropped the issue and instead took it as a 'hard lesson in business partners'. That was until two rough looking gentlemen arrived unannounced at 1308 Wellington Street some weeks later. After brushing their way past a wise-cracking Joe Fagan, and finding their own way up the four stairs, and through the trophy and gift wrapping room and into Howard's private office, these two (who were not from Ottawa as Howard or Joe would have recognized them), explained: i) that they knew Howard had been 'burned'; ii) that they knew how to find the Montreal scammer who did it; and iii) that they had two different cash offers for their services. The first price was to put the Montreal promoter 'in the hospital', and the second price was to 'put him in a box'. A shaken Howard Darwin declined both offers (he had no cash to pay them anyway), and never did hear from these two out-of-towners again.

Even promoting the established formula of the universally loved Harlem Globetrotters basketball show presented risks for Howard. First there was the turnstile stampede of November 1968 when over 12,000 people showed up to watch the Globetrotters at the 10,000 seat Ottawa Civic Centre. Once the tickets ran out, an outdoor ticket booth was turned over by the angry mob who then stormed the gates to get into the sold out arena for free. In 1971, Howard was unlucky once again with the Harlem Globetrotters when he had to cancel his scheduled shows in both London and Ottawa because of the Globetrotters first ever players strike (it cost Howard almost $4,500)! Through it all however, Howard Darwin struck up an unlikely friendship with Harlem Globetrotters star player Meadowlark Lemon, who would send Howard postcards from around the world. Lemon's own secret ambition was to retire from the Globetrotters and to sing in nightclubs - which he was setting Howard up to book for him here in Canada!

In the early 70s, famous motorcycle daredevil Evel Knievel was refused a permit to jump the Grand Canyon in his steam-powered Skycycle X2 rocket. Undeterred, Knievel instead planned a jump of Idaho's Snake River Canyon for a big 1974 closed-circuit television event which - naturally - Howard Darwin presented in Ottawa. Very few paid to watch the jump live in which Knievel crashed and broke his nose. Howard failed and lightened his wallet for his forty-fourth birthday!

In 1972 for example, Howard had to sue two Canadian concert promoters after they took his booking fees and their acts Santana and Sly and the Family Stone to other cities instead. Then there was the time that he had to vouch for the American roadies of the rock band Quiet Riot at the London Gardens when they were detained by the London police for selling tour merchandise without a permit. The Darwin children were handsomely compensated in Quiet Riot concert t-shirts for that one!

(29) Kinsella, Jack: The Ottawa Citizen; pg. xx, Mar 9, 1966

(30) Kealey, Clem: The Ottawa Journal; pg. 15, Au 31, 1971
(31) Louks, Bob: The Ottawa Citizen; pg. 1, Feb 7, 1967
(32) Shero, Fred: Personal Letter; Mar 12, 1967

XIV - ONES THAT GOT AWAY

In later years, Howard Darwin took on some events and roles in his sports and business endeavours that ultimately led to some more taxing personal setbacks - and bigger opportunities foregone.

In the late 70s Howard Darwin faced one of his biggest sports related challenges, and lost badly to the most powerful man in hockey: Alan "The Eagle" Eagleson. As a lawyer, player-agent, international hockey czar and respected hockey advisor to the Canadian government, Eagleson was untouchable in hockey circles around the world at the time. Eagleson's federal crony and fellow piglet at the public trough was a former parliamentarian named Doug Fisher, who was the Chairman of Hockey Canada.

Believing that he was protecting the interests of junior hockey in general, and sensing that Eagleson was now trying to control hockey players from the cradle to the grave for his own benefit, Howard Darwin took the belligerent Eagleson to task when the NHL quit paying development fees to the junior operators for Eagleson represented draftees. Howard also called out Alan Eagleson and Doug Fisher for their questionable use of the public purse for Team Canada at the May 1977 world tournament in Vienna. In another major showdown, Howard outed Eagleson for his player representations of the underage junior hockey players during the WHA raids that threatened all of junior hockey in the 70s.

On September 15, 1977, Howard Darwin was summoned to a Hockey Canada International Committee meeting for the December 1977 World Juniors Tournament to be hosted in Canada. Howard was on the Committee representing junior hockey. The meeting was held in Alan Eagleson's Toronto offices, and Howard was held outside the meeting room for nearly four hours before he was called in and fired from the committee. Howard explained it this way: *"That's what it amounts to. The junior people who will be supplying all the players for the world championships here this winter were just thrown out... They told me that by unanimous vote, I was no longer the junior delegate on the committee, that there would be no junior delegate on the committee, that they would run it."* [33] The backlash from the public and junior hockey in Canada was somewhat critical of the strong arm tactics of Doug Fisher and Alan Eagleson at the time.

Afterwards, a petulant Fisher wrote several defensive letters to the editors of the more derogatory newspapers, and a defiant Eagleson mailed Howard Darwin a personal greeting card with a stylized "KMA" on the outside, and a "Kiss My Ass" greeting inside. Howard kept the card as his 'losers' trophy from their many battles. In a 1979 interview, Eagleson was quoted saying *"We've been at each other's throats a number of times, but it's all passed."* [34] It certainly wasn't over as far as Howard was concerned. Alan Eagleson's personal greed would be the ruin of hockey and Howard Darwin simply hated him for it.

Sighting 'sour grapes' over Howard Darwin's 1977 dismissal from the World Junior Tournament, few in the hockey world chose to side with Howard and his public criticism of Alan Eagleson and Doug Fisher in the 70s or 80s. However by 1992, the NHL players themselves forced Eagleson to step down from the helm of the NHL Players Association over his abuses of their pension and insurance money. Justice for The Eagle was eventually served in 1994 when the FBI charged him with thirty-four counts of racketeering, obstruction of justice, embezzlement and fraud. In Canada, the RCMP finally caught up with Eagleson in 1996 laying eight counts of fraud and theft. Eagleson eventually went to jail and was disbarred from the legal profession. The Eagle had his

Order of Canada rescinded and he was kicked out of the Hockey Hall of Fame. Howard Darwin and his "Kiss My Ass" greeting card were vindicated in the end.

Although Howard Darwin never used the word "bully" to describe Alan Eagleson, hockey legend Bobby Orr eventually used the term (and other critical adjectives) in his 2013 biography, 'Orr – My Story': *"It wasn't just that Eagleson had hidden from me the opportunity to be a part-owner of the Bruins. It was that he had left me practically broke."* [35]

Buoyed by his success in bringing cable television to Ottawa with Ottawa Cablevision Limited, and concerned about technical difficulties with some of his live closed circuit promotions, Howard Darwin seized upon an emerging market for premium and specialty home television, and applied to the Canadian Radio-television and Telecommunications Commission (CRTC) in 1981 for a license to establish an all-sports television network in Canada. The CRTC failed to see the merits of Howard's application and a new television channel like this, and summarily rejected his application. Three years later, the CRTC accepted Labatt Brewing Company's application for The Sports Network (TSN) in 1984. At least the winner that time was Howard Darwin's favourite brand of beer!

Howard also had former 67's play-by-play man Mike Anscombe submit a bid to Ontario Hockey League commissioner Dave Branch to purchase a 10-game pay-per-view deal, which included the league all-star game and nine regular season games on Saturday afternoons from late January to the end of the regular season. The deal was supposed to net the league between $60,000 and $150,000 with Anscombe producing the telecasts. Howard was to get 40 percent of the profits with the league taking 60 percent. The bid was away ahead of its time and the league went instead for years without a legitimate television deal.

About seven months after Conroy Nelson literally disappeared in the middle of the night from Halifax and Howard Darwin's life in 1981, Howard was being offered another chance at taking a promising young Canadian heavyweight professional. This time the request to be a fighter's Manager again was coming from Toronto, and Howard's good friend and retired Canadian boxer, George Chuvalo. Trusting in the former heavyweight great George Chuvalo's instincts, but still reeling from his Conroy Nelson nightmare, Howard took down the name of the prospect and hung up to call his Montreal boxing insider, Roy Hamilton. When Howard connected with Montreal, Roy advised Howard that he was hearing good things about the young prospect but to be aware that this fellow was also from Jamaica – just like Conroy Nelson. It was all the once-burned Darwin needed to hear before he called Chuvalo back and said: "*no thanks!*" George Chuvalo's prospect was named Razor Ruddick, who went on to have a pretty good boxing career including fights with Michael Dokes, Lennox Lewis and Mike Tyson (twice)!

In what Howard Darwin described as his greatest sporting regret, Howard and partner Earl Montagano nearly purchased the NHL's troubled St. Louis Blues hockey team in 1983. During the 1982-1983 season, Blues corporate owner Ralston Purina ran out of patience with the money losing NHL franchise and put it up for sale unconditionally. In January 1983 Ralston Purina accepted an offer from interests in Saskatoon that would have seen the team move into a proposed new arena in Saskatchewan. The NHL blocked the sale however and a bitter legal battle between league president John Ziegler and the pet food giant ensued. There were very few perspective purchasers that would have kept the expansion franchise (a 1967 expansion coincidently - just like the major junior Ottawa 67's) in St. Louis, so Howard and Earl jumped on a plane that summer for the Gateway City.

Howard had no qualms with joining the big league of hockey. Heck, he had dealt with the league from the mid-60s and knew all the owners of the "Original Six" and many of the newer owners and the league grew from six teams to 12, then 14, on its way to the present-day 30. Howard was not intimidated by any of them. But in the summer of 1983, with the Blues bankrupt, this was Howard's chance to play with the big boys. And for many years after, Howard often wondered "what if?" and if maybe he and his partners shouldn't have jumped at it.

Darwin had all the financial information at his disposal. Every expense from cleaning bills to security to the salary of the switchboard operator to the cost of cleaning the parking lot at the Blues home rink "The Checkerdome" to the cost of keeping an ambulance at all home games. Documents show the maintenance people earned $8/hr, the electricians $11.90/hr, matrons (for women's washrooms) $6.75 and that 10 ticket sellers split $320 a game. Police were paid $9.25/hr. Howard broke down all the numbers like no-one else.

"We're just going along at our own speed and putting together whatever information we have," Howard told the St. Louis Post-Dispatch, July 13th, 1983 while in St. Louis to take a first-hand look at things. *"If we get what we want and are satisfied with it, then we will go ahead."*

Howard was also well aware the Blues had too much tied up in contracts for enough players to ice 2 1/2 teams. The entire Blues payroll the previous season (1982-83) was $2.91 million for 21 players with the big team with Bernie Federko the highest paid at $252,000 and Jack Carlson, who was originally supposed to play the third Hanson brother in the epic Slap Shot movie (he was called up to the WHA Edmonton Oilers just as shooting began) at the tail end of the pay scale at $74,000. The roster included one of Howard's favourite 67's in Blake Dunlop, who was earning $150,000, and another favourite in former London Knight in Rob Ramage, at $145,000.

The Blues were on the hook for another $1.2 million for its minor leaguers, a roster that included future Hull Olympiques head coaches Alain Vigneault and Claude Julien. And with 50 players under contracts, there was trimming that would needed to be done. Moving forward, the Blues were on the hook for just $2.7 million in guaranteed salaries at the NHL for the 1983-84 season so the financial outlook did not appear bleak. Add that to the fact the St. Louis people had supported the club with average attendance of 13,000 a game over a 30-year period.

Howard always said the Blues, the Central Hockey League franchise in Salt Lake City and the Checkerdome were all there for the taking. Problem was, the trigger had to be pulled within a week. The NHL needed a deal in place to continue planning for the upcoming season. There was no wiggle room as far as time went.

"We really just ran out of time," remembered Darwin years later. *"But if we could have got everything in order, we could have had it."* Howard had the bid ready. It was going to be himself, Earl and business associate and longtime friend, renowned Ottawa lawyer Gordon Henderson. There was no man on earth Howard trusted more than Mr. Henderson. His

deal was to close on July 28th, 1983. Howard's bid also involved a first right of refusal to move the team to the Seattle-Tacoma, Washington area, if St. Louis did not work out. It was prepared to be sent to NHL legal counsel Gilbert Stein at NHL headquarters in New York City. Howard and Earl held back their offer.

With just ten days to go before the NHL's dissolution date, California vending machine and real estate magnate Harry Ornest (who was raised in Edmonton) stepped up with the only formal purchase offer to be made to the NHL, which was three million in cash plus another nine million in long-term loans from the NHL to purchase the Blues and keep them in St. Louis. Back in Ottawa - and without the full details of the Ornest offer - Howard was already second guessing himself when his lawyer and Ottawa Cablevision partner, Gordon Henderson, called to offer Howard some encouragement. Howard told him *"It's too late Gordon. We were being rushed and we just didn't have that kind of money"*, to which Henderson replied: *"Yes we did Howard"*. The respected Ottawa lawyer would have backed Howard and Earl financially on this one!

After just three years, Harry Ornest sold the Blues and left St. Louis to return to California with a $3.4 million profit on the hockey team, an $8.2 million profit on the arena for a total pre-tax profit on both of $11.6 million. He also left with the unofficial title of the man who saved the St. Louis Blues. The Blues franchise was sold again in 2006 for a whopping $150 million!

Boxing regrets for Howard were not limited to the heavyweight division: *"So there won't be a junior middleweight championship fight at the Civic Centre next month. And that's not through any fault of Howard Darwin. When Howard announced there would be a fight, he believed everything was in order because that's the only way Howard operates. He's first class. Howard is also highly respected by everyone in the professional boxing game. There's no doubt in my mind Howard Darwin will bring Matthew Hilton to Ottawa to defend his title sometime in the very near future."* [36] Unfortunately for Howard and fight fans in Ottawa, he never did get to stage a championship fight in his hometown.

Although he had sold the Ottawa Lynx franchise in 2000, Howard Darwin nonetheless bemoaned the loss of professional baseball in

Ottawa once again, when Ray Pecor's Lynx played their last game in the $16.9 million stadium that he had built and privately paid for on Monday, September 3, 2007. Labour Day was indeed a very sad day for Howard when the Lynx packed up and left for Allentown, Pennsylvania. At one time there were Triple-A baseball teams in Ottawa, Vancouver, Calgary and Edmonton, and now there are no Canadian based teams at the highest levels of professional baseball – other than the (resurgent) Toronto Blue Jays.

(33) MacCabe, Eddie: The Ottawa Citizen; pg. 17, Sep 16, 1977
(34) Elliott, Bob: The Ottawa Citizen; pg. 49, Oct 4, 1979
(35) Orr, Bobby: Orr – My Story; pg. 201, 2013
(36) Charlebois, Marc J.: The Sunday Herald; pg. 13, Jun 26, 1988

XV – THE NEWSBOY AND THE NEWSMEN

Being 'ink-stained' from an early age, it comes as no surprise that Howard Darwin truly enjoyed his relationship with the press, particularly the sportswriters. It may have been because they kept similar late hours or shared common interests and beverages, or that Howard just never declined to comment when they called. And while he was occasionally misquoted or taken out of context, Howard never requested an apology, correction or retraction – except when one city hall reporter printed an August 2006 Mayor Bob Chiarelli quote that he ought to have known was 'seriously inaccurate'. Howard earned a retraction for that one. When newsmen became critical (or accused him of being in the Mob!), he would simply say: *"You catch some bricks when you're catching bouquets"*.

Some radio and television personalities became allies as well, like Dave "The Voice" Schreiber of CFRA, whom Howard convinced in 1981 to call his first and only live radio boxing broadcast of the Trevor Berbick vs. Conroy Nelson Canadian and Commonwealth heavyweight championship from Halifax. Or Global Television news anchor Mike Anscombe, who started in Ottawa covering the Ottawa 67's for CFRA, and who continued to call Howard Darwin regularly – usually late at night – for many years afterwards to keep up with the news from Ottawa. Later on the local television sports 'youngsters' like

Brian Smith, Dan Seguin, Terry Marcotte and Mark Sutcliffe became Howard Darwin supporters too.

None of the close relationships that Howard Darwin had with the journalists came close however, to the reverence that he held for his dear friend, Ottawa Citizen sports writer (and fellow Sherriff's Deputy!) Don Campbell. It was Don Campbell whom Howard treated like a son, likely because "Donnie" would listen with interest, again and again, to Howard's oft-repeated old stories from their familiar reserved seats at the Ottawa Nepean Canadians Sports Club. Don Campbell also made sure that his old friend kept up with his beloved newspapers from around the world – hand delivered to the Darwin's door, right after the Ottawa Citizen was done with them – right up until the day Howard died.

Here then, is a sampling of what some of the Newsmen had to say about the Newsboy over the years:

> *"Howard believes that if professional sport is to be revived, if we are going to get back some of the feature attractions which were so greatly enjoyed in past years, waiting for a strong wind to blow them back into the city is likely to take longer than he's prepared to wait."*
>
> TIMES STAFF: THE OTTAWA TIMES; PG. 2, APR 9, 1958

> *"Thereupon Promoter Howard Darwin, who may be a fall guy for the boxing racket boys down this way, for all I know, booked as a substitute match Gail Kerwin of Valley Stream against Ray Portilla."*
>
> DAN PARKER: THE NEW YORK MIRROR; PG. XX, MAY 30, 1958

> *"Everybody has a secret ambition in life, and by his own admission, Darwin's longstanding aspiration was to promote a world heavyweight championship one day."*
>
> JACK KINSELLA: THE OTTAWA CITIZEN; PG. 19, MAR 9, 1966

"Latest 'big league' touch by Mayor Don Reid and the City Fathers is the Greater Ottawa Sports Hall of Fame... Darwin is in charge of public relations, and the entire operation to date has been a high class one."

JACK KOFFMAN: THE OTTAWA CITIZEN; PG. 13, JAN 17, 1967

"Darwin, who still occasionally gets kidded as the 'boy promoter' because of his youthful appearance, has a substantial string of successes behind him in an extremely short time. Aside from some rather successful ventures in normal business fields, he's made a good go of wrestling and closed-circuit boxing here."

BOB MELLOR: THE OTTAWA CITIZEN; PG. XX, FEB XX, 1967

"So it's the Ottawa 67's. Howard Darwin, the boy genius behind Ottawa's new OHA junior hockey entry, made the pronouncement a few days ago."

BOB MELLOR: THE OTTAWA CITIZEN; PG. XX, JUL 5, 1967

"Howard Darwin is the evergreen optimist. Flexing his watchmaker's muscles to build his case...he convinced us."

EDDIE MACCABE: THE OTTAWA JOURNAL; PG. 13, JAN 20, 1968

"Today, at 40, Darwin isn't an admiral, but he's a wealthy jeweler, promoter, real estate speculator, cablevision magnate and hockey tycoon."

GORD WALKER: THE GLOBE AND MAIL; PG. XX, JAN 27, 1972

"Howard Darwin, who hobnobs with hockey hierarchy at both the pro and amateur level, once referred to player's

agents as 'flesh peddlers'. He's toned down since then and calmly calls them leeches, shysters, carnie hucksters before lapsing into coarser language."

CLEM KEALEY: THE OTTAWA JOURNAL; PG. 18, MAY 24, 1974

"There's Howard Darwin, now linked with the likeable Earl Montagano, trying to make a go of the 67's. Howard always goes first class in everything he does. Howard deserves the best."

JACK KOFFMAN: THE OTTAWA CITIZEN; PG. 18, OCT 30, 1976

"Darwin is both a businessman and a hockey fan. He is too much of a businessman to squander long-term prosperity for short-term gain and too much of a hockey fan to meddle in the activity on the ice."

JOHN VORMITTAG: THE LONDON FREE PRESS; PG. 18, APR 22, 1977

"Darwin equates any business venture with gambling. His mother died when he was five years old and at eight he was on the street hustling newspapers and selling worms. Has success changed Darwin? To most of his friends and associates the answer would be no."

JORDAN JUBY: THE OTTAWA CITIZEN; PG. 19, APR 29, 1977

"Alan Eagleson doesn't like people asking questions about how he goes about his job of looking after Canada's interests in international hockey. He threatened to quit this week when a plebeian by the name of Howard Darwin asked that Alan try just a trifle harder to kinda keep him abreast of what he was doin'."

ERNIE MILLER: THE LONDON FREE PRESS; PG. 17, SEP 9, 1977

"Howard Darwin has been dropped as an international voice, without ever being granted a proper hearing for the upcoming global junior tournament...Darwin had a toy pistol against people who own cannons."

CLEM KEALEY: THE OTTAWA JOURNAL; PG. 17, SEP 16, 1977

"Darwin is a reluctant rich man – not reluctant to be rich, just reluctant to admit it. And he's reluctant to admit to having influence in any of his fields...Newsboys pick up a lot of street smarts and Darwin, a real Harold Robins paperback character, was no exception."

BOB ELLIOT: THE OTTAWA CITIZEN; PG. 49, OCT 4, 1979

"Perhaps it is that sunny enjoyment of unexpected contrasts, coupled with a lack of pretension and a deep concern for the development of the next generation – not only in sports, but as people – that has brought this former newsboy to the pinnacle of the Canadian sports establishment. For integrity and goodness endure. And so will Howard Darwin, Ottawa's own sports czar, to the benefit of all whose lives he has ever touched."

EVA BEDARD: ENTERPRISER MAGAZINE; VOLUME 5, NUMBER 1, PG. 17, DEC 1981

"Howard Darwin dresses well, seldom wears a tie, drinks either Labatt's 50 or Molson's Ex, and spends most weekends on his daughter's farm outside Almonte spoiling his granddaughters."

BOB ELLIOT: THE OTTAWA CITIZEN; PG. D1, DEC 26, 1986

"That sentiment was echoed by the man who landed the junior hockey franchise for Ottawa, Howard Darwin.

Darwin, who outfoxed Sam Berger and others to win the franchise bid, soon wondered if he'd done the right thing."

WAYNE SCANLAN: THE OTTAWA CITIZEN; PG. CI, DEC 29, 1987

"He got there by himself, up by the bootstraps as they used to say, up from nothing. Sure, he had some boosts along the way…but mostly he got there by nerve and guts and savvy. So there is no pretense about Howard Darwin, no affections. He gambled, took his chances, and won more than he lost."

EDDIE MACCABE: THE OTTAWA CITIZEN; PG. BI, DEC II, 1988

"And Darwin, the hockey owner, boxing fan and promoter, budding Triple-A baseball owner and general all-around good guy will probably try to deflect the praise somewhere else. As the owner of the 67's since their inception 23 years ago, Darwin is about as far removed from the Harold Ballards and George Steinbrenners of the world it's not even funny."

DON BRENNAN: THE OTTAWA SUN; PG. 34, MAY 31, 1989

"Howard Darwin doesn't like the limelight. Last night, he couldn't avoid it."

BRUCE GARRIOCH: THE OTTAWA SUN; PG. 36, JUN 1, 1989

"The Darwin theory on The Man himself was discussed many times, many ways this week at the Congress Centre and the Ottawa Nepean Canadians Sports Club. Best put, Howard Darwin is a man's man. He's a rich man, who remembers his roots at the Ottawa Boys Club."

BOB ELLIOTT: THE OTTAWA SUN; PG. 37, JUN X, 1989

> *"You should understand that Darwin is not a man who seeks out headlines. TV makes him jumpy. Publicity makes him shy. If Darwin was a pen, he'd write in invisible ink. You'd never catch him doing a Billy Carter bellyflop just because the cameras were rolling. Darwin's a man moderate in all things, a guy who has made his millions discreetly."*
>
> JANE O'HARA: THE OTTAWA SUN; PG. 35, DEC 5, 1989

> *"Howard Darwin is not a publicity seeker. Anything but. He loves Ottawa, he loves sports, he has the drive, desire and wherewithal to do something about it. To enhance Ottawa's lousy image, to create some fun, to create some employment."*
>
> EARL MCRAE: THE OTTAWA CITIZEN; PG. XX, DEC XX, 1989

> *"With the exception of football, there isn't a major sport in the city untouched by Darwin's entrepreneurial endeavors, and while sports and other business ventures have made Darwin millions, the city as a whole has greatly benefitted from his presence and astute, no-nonsense vision."*
>
> MARK HENDERSON: OTTAWA BUSINESS MAGAZINE; PG. 24, JAN / FEB 1992

> *"You might know Howard Darwin as the affable, determined man who brought junior hockey and Triple-A baseball to Ottawa. But it's the jewelry business that gave Darwin his start, fed the four kids in the early years and allowed him to make his fortunes elsewhere."*
>
> DAVID SCANLAN: THE OTTAWA CITIZEN; PG. XX, MAR XX, 1992

> *"Nicholas Street in 1941 was a noisy, grimy place: slum row-housing beside railway yards, where children roamed while*

adults worked or drank. Its park was a haven for bums and drunks. In this rough atmosphere, 10-year old Howard Darwin was already making a name for himself."

CANADIAN PRESS STAFF: THE LONDON FREE PRESS; PG. D2, SEP 16, 1992

"In this fast-paced, ever-changing world, there remains only a few constants upon which we can truly count. One of them is Howard Darwin."

BARRE CAMPBELL: THE OTTAWA SUN; PG. 51, NOV 27, 1992

"Over the course of 30 years it is Darwin who has become synonymous with sports success in the Nation's Capital. In fact we think it is Darwin who represents all that is good about sports in Ottawa."

JEFFREY MAGUIRE: THE ALMONTE GAZETTE; PG. 4, SEP 20, 1995

"Darwin has a sports and business history in this community spanning nearly five decades. His record for paying bills is first rate."

WAYNE SCANLAN: THE OTTAWA CITIZEN; PG. G1, AUG 23, 1997

"The move also allowed the trustees (of the Ottawa Sports Hall of Fame) to pay homage to Darwin, a humble, spotlight-shy man who brought the local sports scene the Ottawa 67's major junior hockey team and International League baseball's Ottawa Lynx."

MARTIN CLEARY: THE OTTAWA CITIZEN; PG. F2, SEP 1, 1998

"Yet this same Howard Darwin, who wove together so much of the fabric of Ottawa's sporting life in the second

half of the 20*th* century, has also been generous and kind to the disadvantaged; a principled builder of athletic pursuits and the venues to house them; a charming, gentle and handsome man. He might be the best friend the local sports community has known."

WAYNE SCANLAN: THE OTTAWA CITIZEN; PG. E1, DEC 26, 1999

"The name Howard Darwin has become synonymous with sport in Ottawa, with a roller-coaster career that runs from jewelry to baseball diamonds. Howard was the classic entrepreneur – a risk taker who put his own money up front."

PAT MACADAM: THE OTTAWA SUN; PG. 4, DEC 15, 2002

"It's funny he went for the wrestling programs first. Darwin is the man who brought us the Ottawa 67's and the Ottawa Lynx. The same guy who booked bands like Joey Dee and the Starlighters – 'direct from the Peppermint Lounge' – and Sly and the Family Stone. Fifty years of being a sports and entertainment promoter, with filing cabinets full of memorabilia, but he's a sucker for the 'wrasslers'."

RON CORBETT: THE OTTAWA SUN; PG. 5, MAR 3, 2008

"Howard Darwin, one of Ottawa's foremost sportsmen and a true sporting legend far beyond the city limits, died Thursday morning from complications stemming from heart surgery 61 days ago."

DON CAMPBELL: THE OTTAWA CITIZEN; PG. B1, OCT 23, 2009

"His passing signals another shift away from a simpler time when the Ottawa sports community was a village.

Howard Darwin was its heart. Howard was a do-er and a fixer, a helper to underprivileged kids, perhaps because he'd been one, a visionary who made money because he saw the future of real estate and cable TV."

    WAYNE SCANLAN: THE OTTAWA CITIZEN; PG. A1, OCT 23, 2009

"Howard Darwin was looked at as both one of the most respected and successful men in the room, and, at the same time, as one of the boys."

    DON BRENNAN; THE OTTAWA SUN; PG. 4, OCT 23, 2009

"No one who lived such a colourful life should be so humble – but that was Howard, brokering million-dollar deals with lords of enterprise then sitting down to a beer with ordinary working men."

    WAYNE SCANLAN: THE OTTAWA CITIZEN; PG. A2, OCT 23, 2009

"He lived modestly with his fabulous wife Connie, and the street urchin never said goodbye to his heart and soul. There was nothing pretentious about Howard Darwin. He was an everyday, ordinary guy most comfortable in the company of everyday, ordinary people of modest means and tastes and interests, drinking beer, talking sports, kibitzing, favouring the unadorned language and visceral rhythms from the streets of his childhood. Howard Darwin was real."

    EARL MCRAE: THE OTTAWA SUN; PG. 4, OCT 23, 2009

"Ottawa never raised a more naturally enterprising individual than Howard Darwin. He often said his success

was due to luck, but it was his tenacity and his integrity that led him from one winner to another."

MARK SUTCLIFFE: THE OTTAWA CITIZEN; PG. DI, OCT 24, 2009

"Howard – whose pockets would acquire millions of self-made bucks, but whose common-man soul retained only pennies – ran a small watch/clock-repair business."

EARL MCRAE: THE OTTAWA SUN; PG. 5, OCT 27, 2009

"He was a realistic, hard-working, clever, persistent local business pioneer with an uncommon integrity, loyalty and community spirit. And Darwin did all of that while remaining the same person who grew up among the tough characters of Nicholas Street."

MARTIN CLEARY: THE OTTAWA CITIZEN; PG. C3, OCT 27, 2009

APPENDIX A

AWARDS & RECOGNITION

1977	Queen Elizabeth II Silver Jubilee Medal
1989	Sportsman of the Year: Ottawa Nepean Canadians Sports Club
1992	Business Person of the Year: Ottawa Carleton Board of Trade
1992	Confederation of Canada 125th Anniversary Medal
1993	Baseball Person of the Year: Kiwanis Club of Ottawa
1993	Guardsman Award: Ottawa Tourism
1995	Business Pioneer of Ottawa: Central Canada Exhibition Association
1995	Executive of the Year: National Association of Professional Baseball Leagues
1995	Village Reunion Contribution Award
1996	Civic Pride Award: City of Ottawa
1998	Earl Bullis Achievement Award: Associated Canadian Travelers (ACT)
1998	Inducted into the Ottawa Sports Hall of Fame
2000	Ottawa Sport Figures of the Century: 7th Place
2009	Lifetime Contribution: Ottawa Sports Awards
2010	Memorial Ten Count: Ringside For Youth XVI
2012	Howard Darwin Centennial Arena Renamed

JEFF DARWIN

OTTAWA BUSINESS MAGAZINE

JANUARY/FEBRUARY 1992 $2.00

HEAVY HITTER
HOWARD DARWIN STRIKES AGAIN

THE INVENTING GAME
TURNING IDEAS INTO PROFITS AND LOSSES

INCORPORATING THE OTTAWA-CARLETON BOARD OF TRADE'S BYWORD

Howard Darwin

Well known on both the Ottawa-Carleton business and sporting scenes, Howard Darwin's long history of contributions to our community make him a very worthy recipient of the Ottawa-Carleton Board of Trade's 1992 Award for Independent Business Person of the Year.

Most recently, Mr. Darwin has garnered headlines for his successful campaign to bring Triple A baseball to the National Capital Region. Next year, the Ottawa Lynx of the International League, the Montreal Expos top-level farm team, will begin competing for Triple A supremacy and jobs in the big leagues in their impressive new home on Coventry Road. Judging from the success and relative youth of the Expos, we are sure to witness high calibre baseball for many years.

Mr. Darwin's success in launching the Lynx has been due to those qualities that have been his hallmarks throughout his life: determination, patience and quiet good humor. Beginning very early in life, Mr. Darwin's success has been all of his own making. Through hard work and creativity, he has succeeded in many different endeavours: jewellery, cablevision, commercial real estate, wrestling promoter, junior hockey and now baseball.

His first business was a jewellery store- an enterprise he began in 1945 and closed only last spring in order to concentrate on his other ventures. But never one to rest on his laurels, the lure of the sports world soon captured him and he began promoting a wide variety of events.

This interest grew into his own Centennial project— the Ottawa 67's. Landing this franchise convinced the City to build the Civic Centre. Mr. Darwin has been owner of the 67's for all 25 years of their history, including their Memorial Cup championship in 1984.

In 1968, he also purchased, with partner, Claude Bennett, the London Knights and their home, the London Gardens. He sold the team in 1987.

Along the way, Mr. Darwin began investing in commercial real estate, first in Ottawa, and later farther afield. In the 60's, Mr. Darwin was also one of the first proponents of cable television in Ottawa.

Despite all this success, Mr. Darwin remains modest and unassuming. The excitement of bringing a new project to fruition keeps him motivated. Happy and unpretentious, Howard Darwin is certain to be a major player on the Ottawa-Carleton scene for many years to come.

In Memoriam – Howard Darwin

Howard Darwin – 1930-2009

Triple-A baseball, the Ottawa 67's – sports in Ottawa owes much to Howard Darwin. His generosity of spirit and strong sense of community has left an indelible mark on this city. His inspired entrepreneurial ability launched cablevision in Ottawa. His love of sports brought junior hockey to the city and provided the incentive to build the Ottawa Civic Centre. He brought baseball to the capital. His love of the 'sweet science' led him into promoting boxing locally and on closed-circuit TV. He was a friend of the Boys and Girls Club and a generous supporter of Ringside for Youth. It is our privilege to honour Howard Darwin this evening and to say thank you for the legacy he has left this city.

Howard Darwin
Memorial Scholarships (est. 2009)

Howard Darwin was one of the most highly-regarded and influential members of the Ottawa Sports Community ever and his impact spanned half a century and continues today. Mr. Darwin brought Major Junior A Hockey to the capital with the Ottawa 67's. He returned professional baseball to the region with the AAA Ottawa Lynx. He promoted professional wrestling and boxing throughout Eastern Canada and was a driving force behind the Ottawa Beaver Boxing Club, one of the most successful amateur clubs in North America. He was also an irreplaceable force behind the Ottawa Nepean Canadians Sports Club.

At the time of his passing, the Sports Club, in conjunction with the directors of the Ottawa Sports Awards, sought a manner is which to recognize Howard's commitment to amateur sports and introduced the Howard Darwin Memorial Athletic Scholarships.

To date, $10,000 in scholarships have been awarded.

Congratulations to all of tonight's winners and guests and best of luck to the scholarship winners in pursuit of their athletic dreams.

Best wishes from Connie Darwin and the Darwin family, Ottawa Nepean Canadians President Rob Clouthier, the Directors of the Club, and its more than 300 members and patrons.

Year	Male Student Athlete	Female Student Athlete
2013	Ben Wilkenson-Zam - Cross Country Ski	Madeline Schmidt - Canoe/Kayak Sprint
2012	John Wright - Fencing	Gillian Baggott - Soccer
2011	Eric Kemp - Orienteering	Grace Lonergan - Softball
2010	Robbie Anderson - Orienteering	Rachel Homan - Curling
2009	Ben Hayward - Canoe/Kayak White Water	Kristin Gauthier - Canoe/Kayak Sprint

APPENDIX B

PHOTO CREDITS
(CHAPTER - PHOTO NUMBER)

All published photos in The Ten Count are Darwin Family Photos, except for those listed below:

CHI-2	Lost Ottawa via Facebook (pg. 5)
CHI-3	City of Ottawa Archives CA008108 (pg. 5)
CHII-1	Ottawa Boys Club via Twitter (pg. 16)
CHII-2	Past Ottawa via Facebook (pg. 16)
CHII-4	City of Ottawa Archives CA006742 (pg. 16)
CHII-5	Traversy Family Photo (pg. 16)
CHII-6	Past Ottawa via Facebook (pg. 17)
CHII-9, 10	Lost Ottawa via Facebook (2x, pg. 17)
CHIV	Lost Ottawa via Facebook (1x, pg. 41)
CHIV	Lost Ottawa via Facebook (2x, pg. 43)
CHIV	Lost Ottawa via Facebook (1x, pg. 44)
CHV	City of Ottawa Archives CA018343 (pg. 52)
CHV	City of Ottawa Archives CA024845, CA007004, CA024847J (pg. 56)
CHVII	Lost Ottawa via Facebook (2x, pg. 79)
CHVIX	Riley88 Cartoon (pg. 104: Sunday Herald; Jun 26, 1988, pg. 13)

CHVIX	City of Ottawa Archives CA002357 (pg. 106)
PG.166	Cover from Ottawa Business Magazine Jan / Feb 1992
PG.167	Program page from the Ottawa-Carleton Business Person of the Year Awards 1992
PG.168	Program page from Ringside For Youth XVI (2010)
PG.169	Program page from the Ottawa Sport Awards 2014

APPENDIX C

PEOPLE AND PLACES
(PAGE FIRST MENTIONED)

A

Ages, Saul	65
Albion Hotel	36
Ali, Mohammed	90
Andre the Giant	65
Andrews, Shane	122
Anka, Paul	138
Anscombe, Mike	100
Armstrong, Louis	12
Arum, Bob	140
Aubry, Dr. Mark	133
Aucoin, Derek	122

B

Barber, Gerry	9
Barlow, Gilbert	30
Barre Sisters	9
Barry, Carl	30
Beatles, The	74

Beaver Barracks	20
Beaver Boxing Club	26
Bedard, Eva	157
Bennett, Claude	67
Bennett, Tony	112
Berbick, Trevor	97
Berger, Sam	82
Berry, Jack	9
Berry, Jimmy "Irish"	9
Boivin, Leo	89
Boston, Steve	111
Bowerman, Jack	54
Branch, Dave	109
Brennan, Don	158
Britannia Beach	2
Brochu, Claude	110
Bronfman, Charles	110
Brower, Dick "Bulldog"	64
Brown, David	78
Bryck, John	120
Bull, Bobby	131
Burke, Miss	7
Burke, Tim	36
Butterworth, Alan	82

C

Calcutt, Ernie	82
Cameron, Effie	2
Cameron Highlanders of Ottawa	13
Campbell, Barre	123
Campbell, Don	63
Campeau Construction	62
Camp Minwassin	2
Carleton County Jail	35
Carlson, Jack	149
Cash, Johnny	102

Cassina, Loren	73
Chandler, Jeff	63
Charbonneau, Arnie	22
Charlebois, Marc J.	151
Chiarelli, Bob	153
Chouinard, Gilbert	54
Chow, Dr. Don	133
Chuvalo, George	100
Chynoweth, Ed	103
Ciccarelli, Dino	89
Clarke, J. J.	131
Clay, Cassius	74
Clement, Bill	84
Cleary, Martin	163
Clyde, Ian	99
Coghlan, Eileen	23
Connelly, Nola	11
Connelly, Violet & Bill	11
Cooney, Gerry	102
Corbett, Ron	161
Cosenzo, Frankie	9
Cowley, Bill	82
Cregan, Lenny "Snake"	117
Curry, Mrs.	9

D

Darmont Holdings	84
Darwin's Watch Clinic	47
Darwin, Connie	4
Darwin, Howard	1
Darwin, Jack (brother)	2
Darwin, Jack (son)	63
Darwin, Jeff	63
Darwin, Johanna	26
Darwin, Josephine	4
Darwin, Kim	60

Darwin, Marie "Mayme"	1
Darwin, Nancy	60
Darwin, Percy	2
Darwin, Rupert	2
Darwin, Vincent	3
Davey, Keith	81
Davis, Earl "Smokey"	9
Diamond BBQ	65
Diefenbaker, John	90
Donovan, Shean	91
Dows Lake	47
Drinkwater, Bill and June	49
Dryden, Steve	103
Dunlop, Blake	88
Dunphy, Don	62
Dupas, Davey "The Whip"	61
Durrell, Jim	110
Dutchie's Hole	10

E

Eagleson, Alan	145
Elliot, Bob	151

F

Fagan, Joe	61
Father Connolly	49
Federko, Bernie	149
Feller, Bobby	59
Ferguson, Bob	v
Fisher, Doug	145
Foo, Doug	4
Frayne, Trent	29

G

Gamble, Don	116
Gandhi, Mahatma	20
Garland & Mutchmore	76
Garrioch, Bruce	158
Gatineau Club	50
Gayle, Greg	99
Gervais, Dave	110
Gittens, Dr. Rudy	128
Goff, Robert	99
Gorman, Tommy	50
Gosselin, Jack	131
Goudie, Connie	45
Goudie, Gerry	48
Goudie, Irene	48
Goulet Family	4
Gouzenko, Igor	35
Graham, Dr. Jerry	64
Graham, Tim	103
Gray Rocks	92
Gretzky, Walter	101
Grudzielanek, Mark	122

H

Hamilton, Gord	89
Hamilton, Roy	148
Haney, Todd	122
Harris, Roy	62
Harlem Globetrotters	143
Harvey, Bruce	39
Henderson, Gordon	75
Henderson, Mark	123
Henry, Howard	74
Herbert, John	92
Hilton, Matthew	150

Holmes, Larry	98
Hospodar, Ed	91
Hotel Laurier	11
Howard Darwin Jewellers	59
Hunt, Jeff	103
Hunter, Bill	148
Hutchison, Dave	88

I

Ink Spots Band	50

J

Johnson, Harry	19
Juby, Jordan	156
Julien, Claude	149

K

Kardish Delicatessen	89
Kealey, Clem	144
Keeping, Max	131
Kelly, Larry	103
Kenny, Clayton	26
Kent, Darrell	117
Kerwin, Gale "Flash"	26
Kielty, Terry	82
Kilrea, Brian	89
King, Don	102
Kinsella, Jack	83
Knievel, Evel	143
Koffman, Jack	92
Kuhlman, Kathryn	90

L

Lacelle Brothers	25
Lacelle, Harvey	25

Laframboise, Peter	108
Lamoureux, Butch	9
Landsdowne Park	20
Lapointe, Charlie	43
Larment, Eugene	35
Laurier House	38
Lebreton Flats	45
Lee, Derek	122
Lee, Peter	91
Legault, Jeff	59
Leikin, Harry	76
Lemon, Meadowlark	143
Lewis, Gerry-Lee	138
Lewis, Stanley	23
Lindsay, Eddie	9
Lindsay, Jack	9
Liston, Sonny	74
Loftus, Jackie	49
London Gardens	86
London Knights	86
London Nationals	86
Long, Bill	83
Louis, Joe "The Brown Bomber"	12
Louks, Bob	144

M

MacAdam, Pat	77
MacCabe, Edward	66
Mackenzie King, William Lyon	14
Mackanin, Pete	122
MacLeod, Robert	103
Maguire, Jeffrey	160
Maloney, Dave	121
Maloney, Tom	119
Maple Leaf Gardens	86
Marcotte, Terry	154

Marsh, Brad	89
Martin, Terence	123
Maruk, Dennis	89
Massie, Johnny	138
McAuley, James	74
McCann, Fred	2
McCormick, Gord	109
McCreery, Christopher	39
McDonald, Ken	142
McIntyre, Wayne	110
McRae, Earl	15
Meehan, Carol Anne	131
Mellor, Bob	83
Merrikin, Al	82
Metrilla, Herbie	54
Miller, Ernie	156
Mobley, Randy	117
Montagano, Earl	26
Montagano, Gordie	26
Montreal Expos	118
Moran, Mike	108
Morrison Lamothe Bakery	49
Mudd, Robert	99

N

National War Memorial	13
Nelles, Percy	13
Nelson, Conroy	97
Nicholas Street	2
Novak, Kim	60

O

O'Brien, Bert	89
O'Brien, Roy	76
O'Leary, Carl "Bates"	9
O'Hara, Jane	159

Ornest, Harry	150
Orr, Bobby	147
O'Sullivan, Shawn	99
Ottawa Athletics	50
Ottawa Auditorium	45
Ottawa 67's	83
Ottawa Boys Club	1
Ottawa Cablevision Limited	76
Ottawa Citizen	13
Ottawa Civic Centre	82
Ottawa Coliseum	73
Ottawa Journal	13
Ottawa Lynx	115
Ottawa Nepean Canadians Sports Club	20
Ottawa Rough Riders	50
Ottawa Sports Hall of Fame	81

P

Pagé, Pierre	123
Pang, Darren	91
Parker, Dan	154
Patterson, Floyd	62
Peca, Mike	91
Plante Bath	46
Post, Paddy	9
Potvin, Armand	85
Potvin, Denis	84
Potvin, Jean	85
Pratt, Doug	87
Pride, Curtis	122

Q

Quarry, Jerry	141
Quade, Michael	119
Quiet Riot	143

R

Ramage, Rob	89
Reid, Don	75
Rheaume, Dorothy	60
Rideau Canal	2
Rideau Club	37
Roberts, Gary	91
Robinson, "Sugar Ray"	26
Rogers Communications	77
Rollocks, Stafford	111
Ruddick, Razor	148
Rueter, Kirk	122
Rupert, Bob	78

S

Sampan Restaurant	83
Sandulo, Joey	26
Santangelo, F. P.	122
Santana	143
Selkirk Communications	76
Scanlan, David	159
Scanlan, Wayne	92
Schmalz, Clarence "Tubby"	88
Schmeling, Max	12
Schreiber, Dave	153
Schultz, Dave	85
Seguin, Dan	154
Shanahan, Brendan	89
Shero, Fred "The Fog"	142
Shorey, Henry	30
Siddall, Joe	123
Simpson, Bobby	130
Sinatra, Frank	60
Sinatra, Nancy	60
Sitler, Darryl	88

Sky Low Low	64
Slapshot Movie	91
Sly and the Family Stone	143
Smith, Bobby	91
Smith, Brian	154
Spratt, Ken	67
Standish Hall	50
Stairs, Matt	121
Stephen-Harvey Jewellers	39
St. Joseph's Boys School	7
St. Joseph's Church	4
St. Louis Blues	148
St. Patrick's High School	36
Stone, Avatus	50
Stoneman, Thomas	35
Sutcliffe, Mark	154
Swartman, Mel	25
Szigetti, John	77

T

Terrell, Ernie	141
Terrible Ted	65
Thivierge, Marie "Mayme"	4
Thomas, Reggie	89
Thompson, Doug "Pops"	19
Touhey, Bill	36
Traversy, Norman	12
Treasure Island Shopping Centre	87
Trombley, Leonard	130
Tucker, Whit	103
Tunney, Frank	109
Tyson, Mike	99

U

Ungerman, Irving	102
Union Station	2

University of Ottawa	23

V

Vien, Donat	82
Vieux, Mrs.	4
Vigneault, Alain	149
Village Reunion Dinner	132
Villeneuve, Armand	54
Vormittag, John	156

W

Walk the Line Movie	102
Wallace House	45
Walker, Gord	155
Watson, Jim	110
Watson, "Whipper" Billy	71
Westwick, Bill	82
Weyburn, HMCS	24
Whelan, Father John	67
White, Rondell	122
Whitton, Charlotte	51
Wilson, Doug	91
Wilson, Murray	108
Winston, Iris	4

X, Y, Z

Zubray, Nick	107

ACKNOWLEDGEMENTS

This biography would not have been possible without the remarkable clarity of recall – often going back over seventy years - as provided by my incredible Mom, Connie. Also, one of my Dad's closest friends in later life was sportswriter Don Campbell, who has been a significant contributor to this book. Lastly, this book's title The Ten Count and the boxing analogy both belong to my beautiful daughter, Allie. *"See you in church!"*

— JEFF M. DARWIN

CPSIA information can be obtained at www.ICGtesting.com
Printed in the USA
LVOW10s0533311215

468236LV00011B/37/P